Combining his successful career as a professional musician, (featuring tours, TV and film, radio, and session work) with his academic profile within higher education, Paul continues to enjoy his musical and creative journey. Alongside his performance and educating duties, Paul is also the co-inventor of The Pegmate—a revolutionary tuning aid for orchestral stringed instruments. Having had musical works and books published, he now extends his portfolio with *Driving a Cat to Portugal and Building a House When We Get There*.

When not 'music-ing!' Paul can be found watching his favoured sport of Rugby League.

To C

To M

Together

Paul Francis

Driving a Cat to Portugal and Building a House When We Get There

AUSTIN MACAULEY PUBLISHERS™
LONDON · CAMBRIDGE · NEW YORK · SHARJAH

Copyright © Paul Francis 2024

The right of Paul Francis to be identified as author of this work has been asserted by the author in accordance with sections 77 and 78 of the Copyright, Designs and Patents Act 1988.

All rights reserved. No part of this publication may be reproduced, stored in a retrieval system, or transmitted in any form or by any means, electronic, mechanical, photocopying, recording, or otherwise, without the prior permission of the publishers.

Any person who commits any unauthorised act in relation to this publication may be liable to criminal prosecution and civil claims for damages.

All of the events in this memoir are true to the best of author's memory. The views expressed in this memoir are solely those of the author.

A CIP catalogue record for this title is available from the British Library.

ISBN 9781035834167 (Paperback)
ISBN 9781035834174 (ePub e-book)

www.austinmacauley.co.uk

First Published 2024
Austin Macauley Publishers Ltd®
1 Canada Square
Canary Wharf
London
E14 5AA

Thanks to all those at Austin Macauley Publishers. Thanks to all those who made this move easier than it could have been.

Let's Move to Portugal

Me: "I've just thought of the opening line."

As I said that, I realised my wife was more interested in the conversation that was happening at the table across from us. A group of OAPs, with one particular couple, were describing how they had parked their car in a restaurant car park—a restaurant where they had enjoyed their meal—only to realise that, when they had returned to their car, the catalytic converter had been stolen.

My opening line had paled into insignificance, as my wife was more intrigued (OK, downright amused) at the fact that it was just as important for the couple to mention they had enjoyed their meal!

We were in the Pink Elephant in Meltham, near Huddersfield, West Yorkshire, England; a restaurant with an excellent seafood platter starter, served on a sizzling bed of char-grilled onions. I decided to follow that with a Chicken and King Prawn Pathia. For my pescatarian wife, an equally tasty prawn thing.

This restaurant had often played host to our strategic, but more often, idealistic conversations about firstly, whether it would be good to move abroad (you'll find out that we thought that was a good idea); secondly, could we afford to do it? (At the time of writing, the jury is still out. We were hoping they consider not only the facts, but also whether to have a whip round on our behalf.) And thirdly, what's stopping us? (We couldn't answer that one.)

I digress. We were out having a meal and, based on our experiences, discussing the merits of starting some sort of blog (hence the necessity for an opening line) detailing the process we encountered when considering, and then deciding to move to Portugal.

If you are reading this, then you have maybe decided on, or at least thought about, the prospect of moving to another country. We thought about it and tried to find reasons why it would not be possible. After much deliberation, largely based on the fact that unless my wife was under direct sunlight then for her, it was a bit chilly, we decided to move to Portugal.

The comparisons that may be drawn between my wife and a lizard had been noted, examined, dismissed and, if I remember the words correctly, "shall not be spoken of again!"

There were times during this process that, perhaps due to a paranoia stemming from the magnitude of what we were doing, and being keen not to fall victim to an illicit Anglo-Portuguese land buying scheme, leading to an appearance in a TV documentary focusing on the perils of buying land or property abroad, we were not always the easiest clients to deal with.

There were no regrets about this, and we had no TV appearances planned. Right now, with the benefit of credible legal advice, we bought some land in the hilltops of Sao Bras de Alportel. São Brás de Alportel is a town and municipality in the District of Faro.

Unlike other perhaps more well-known Algarvian destinations renowned for their attraction to tourists, e.g., Albufeira, Sao Bras is an all-year-round town with Portuguese and incomers enjoying some of the more traditional aspects of Portugal's cultural heritage.

Its population, of about 11,000 residents, enjoy a central Algarvian location, with beaches, the airport and the countryside all within easy reach and this was one of the attractions for us. To be honest though, my wife did the research for all that and I just said OK. Once again, her taste for choosing good things came to the fore.

Although not the first ones we spoke to, sourced through word on the street, Google and general, 'I'm looking for an architect, can you help,' type questions, we had an architect. We didn't realise it at the time but the time it took for us to find the right one was a hint as to the patience we would need for this whole, *bright idea* about moving abroad. For those architects who quoted squillions, thank you for your time.

You join us as:

A. My wife has secured a job in Portugal.
B. Our home in England is for sale.

We have 3D images of our proposed new house. In an ideal world, A+B would equal C. Unfortunately, at this point, A and B are getting on famously. C however, as its primary strategy, has furtive and hopeful glances towards the jury's decision on whether or not to have a whip round.

While we waited for the outcome of deliberations, we kept planning, dreaming and not mentioning lizards.

Why Portugal?

It was my wife who first mentioned the idea of moving to Portugal. She had visited there when she was 17 (a long time ago). "Portugal was very different then," she told me and, as I remember it, she didn't get further than Porto-ish, but still, she did remember (and this is apparently for no particular reason, unless there was something she is hiding) liking it and wanting to return.

For me, I knew there was a place called Portugal, but had never been there, never particularly wanted to go there, but always wondered where the place 'Faro' was when I was at the airport going somewhere else.

Fast forward a few years, more than 20 to be a little bit more exact, during which there was a chance meeting (which for her was love at first sight), a second meeting (when I actually noticed her), a romance, more romance (where some annoying habits started to develop and get noticed), the decision to move in together (so we could start to develop other properties), an acceptance on my part that I had to get on with her cat, Marli (not sure if the cat ever quite took to me).

A decision to rent out some of those properties (I probably won't get around to telling you about the tenants from hell, the missing rent, trashed houses and cannabis factory), the buying of our first house together (which we could easily afford), the buying of our second house together (that we quite simply could not afford, especially as the financial crash happened in the same week we moved in), several holidays (all of which were her idea because I, 'don't really like holidays'; I do now).

The putting off a marriage (because we couldn't be bothered with the fuss), a marriage (in Vegas, and yes, with Elvis), a few more holidays, and it was when at the airport for one of these holidays, I asked, "Where's Faro?"

To which my wife answered, "Portugal, I went there once and it was really nice, I'd like to go back one day." Then at some point, there was a discussion about our next holiday. "Do you fancy Portugal?" my wife asked.

To which I answered, "yeah, whatever," then without a hint of sarcasm (OK, that last bit might not be true) I added, "as long as I'm with you darling." (My reply *may* have warranted my wife's hand gesture).

Anyway, we took a flight to Albufeira around Christmas time (we always go away at Christmas, less fuss), a hotel room with a balcony overlooking the beach (we had a row about something I can't quite remember now, but I'm sure I was right), then we realised Albufeira wasn't for us (although we liked Portugal and the Algarve) and finally, a decision, "We should move to Portugal," (a decision that I'm claiming).

If you are wondering why Portugal, the answer is, as my wife put it, "because it's not Spain." I suppose at this point, I should tell you a little bit more about us. We are forty-somethings, well at least I will be for a bit longer yet.

We have no children because we never wanted any, although getting people to believe that was sometimes harder than getting my wife to admit that there may be a possibility that she could be wrong.

My wife is a professional violinist, music teacher, wicked cook, keen gardener, and a 5 foot 2 and a half inch bundle of energy who is fully charged as day breaks but come 9pm (it's actually closer to 8.30pm) she is adamant that she was not asleep on the sofa and had seen every minute of the gripping series we had planned to watch together.

I am a drummer and a composer who likes to eat what my wife cooks, likes having a nice garden, likes rugby league and who has an appreciation for (I was going to put beer, but I thought that might not tell the whole story) the sweet pairing of food with alcoholic beverages.

I don't think I've actually told you the real reason why Portugal, but where we lived in England, as the train was not practical, I had a regular 3-hour commute to work by car (on the worst days that could be up to 4 hours). One of the most annoying things about that 120-mile journey was that the first 105 miles could take 1 hour and 30 minutes. The next 15 miles could take one hour and 30 plus.

The city is the birthplace of the members of Duran Duran and so during the journeys, I often found myself singing, *please tell me now, is there something I should know? That will make my journeys that little bit less stressful and time consuming.* (I know the last bit doesn't quite scan).

My wife's commute could mean being stuck in traffic for hours for a journey that was approximately 15 miles long and should take about 35 minutes. I often got a phone call while she was on the M62 (hands free of course) that started, "Hi yah, I bloody hate the M62."

We both wanted to be able to continue working in the UK, while developing other working options, but neither of us wanted to continue being stuck in traffic. Where could we possibly live that would allow us to readily predict our travelling time, not have to drive while travelling and yet, enjoy the ever-increasing nature of working from home, a warmer climate and not having to pay 7 or 8 pounds for a pint?

I think I've just told you why we chose Portugal. On top of that, we were ready for something new and every time we visited, we liked it and couldn't explain why, except for the freshly grilled fish (pescatarian wife, you see), fantastic beaches, very little traffic, great weather and, if it's good enough for Cliff Richard, then count us in.

Things Take Time
This Is Portugal

So here we are at a new start for our journey towards moving to Portugal. We made contact with a lawyer who helped us secure the land. We met her associates at one of those exhibition weekends that were often hosted in England.

I'm sure you know the sort of thing, full of trades and companies all trying to sell you something, each one offering a magazine, catalogue or handout that you take to be polite, or fully intend to read.

Either way, before any reading gets done, you look at the pictures, then put them on the first flat surface you come to when you get home (leading to the inevitable, usually said by my wife), "have you finished with these?" Or "are you going to read these?" And finally, "can these be thrown in the bin?"

Anyway, we met a lawyer, she seemed on the ball, we took her details and she took ours. We Googled her, she was well-known and positively reviewed. She had more to lose, in terms of her reputation, than we had to give her, in terms of our hard-earned savings.

We chatted via Skype and, with a bit more research, we felt that we could trust her to work towards our best interests. We were right, so from December 2017 to July 2018, we had made the decision to move abroad, bought land and were popping champagne corks, toasting to, well I'm sure you can imagine.

The fact we had managed to do so much in just a few months meant that when discussing our plans with the many expats (*or should that be immigrants? I'm not sure why the word 'expat' is used for some people, but the word 'immigrant' is used for others*) we had encountered, contacted, met for coffee, etc. (all of whom had given us a warm welcome) and we heard the phrase, "Things take time. This is Portugal."

We just thought, why should that be the case? The Portuguese professionals we had worked with so far went at our pace and after all, we were the proud owners of land in Portugal, go-getter types, we'd be fine.

Our ideas for what we wanted to do with the land included providing homes for two goats (Curry and Ackee). My wife wanted more, but I had to explain that due to Rocky and Adrian (two pigs that, by the time you read the last instalment of this thing, I so hope I'm going to have), there wouldn't be room.

My wife had also mentioned; chickens, alpacas, llamas, geese and, if I remember (then chose to forget) a few other things. Remembering Old McDonald (with his farm and all), E, I, E, I, O is not quite me. I'm more of a kicking groove, phat Bass line and serious melodies kind of guy, so watch this space to see if that changes (good luck with that one).

Either way, needless to say, there were going to be animals and, despite what seemed like an homage to the Pips (Gladys Knight's *Midnight Train to Georgia* backing singers), everywhere we went, we heard and felt the

Portuguese groove, with what seemed like well-meaning backing vocalists singing, "Things take time. This is Portugal."

Meanwhile, we wanted to build two separate dwellings on, 'Our land in Portugal!' This seemed simple enough to us and after all, we had a plan. Whoo, whoo!

July 2019 and our much improved (and increasingly revised) plan was moving forward. We thought that by now, not only would we have concrete answers for those increasingly annoying, 'how's the move to Portugal going?' questions from everyone who knew, or had since found out we were moving, we also thought that we would have some concrete being poured into earth, and dug with the help of my trusty shovel (which I was yet to purchase). We thought that we would finally have the chance for the literal use of the cliché, 'we are pouring money down a hole'.

Alas, that pleasure still awaits us. In reality, we had architect plans, were developing relationships with a new lawyer (the first one was excellent, but we decided to go with someone more local to our land) and were in the process of meeting builders and construction experts.

Hosted by our favourite curry restaurant back home and fuelled by, 'oh go on then, might as well', our vision for what we thought we wanted was now more than a collection of date night conversations. Instead, it was a developing reality.

To get us this far, we have had several trips to Portugal (signing forms, excuses just to go, job interviews, getting the lay of the land), with each one filled with a heady mix of a lack of confidence, an over confidence, frustration, excitement, idealism and anxiety.

What follows is just a snapshot of some of the conversations we've had with each other and with others:

"Let's visit the land, make sure it's still there."
No reply, just a shake of the head (I'll leave you to guess who did and said what).

"I hope the architect can remember the thing we thought was incredibly important at the time that we forgot to tell them when we last saw them that we eventually did tell them that we now can't remember."

Wife: "How are we gonna decide if the builders we're meeting are just a bunch of cowboys?"
Me: "We'll look for the horses." (I thought that was quite funny. I was wrong.)

"What do you think of the new lawyer?"
"I like him."
"Me too."
"Do you think we can trust him?"
"He came recommended and so far, he has been excellent."
"He was late though."
"I know, I hate lateness."

Me: "Why do the council want that?"
Me: "Have we got that?"

"Bearing in mind you are presumably dealing with these types of things all the time, and you said you would call us back and you haven't, why don't you know, and how long will it take you to find out?"

"Well, didn't you ask them?"
"No. I forgot."
"What do you mean you forgot? How could you forget that?"

"Why do you not know when the council will respond to your email?"
"Because they didn't tell me when they were going to respond."
"Did you ask?"
"Yes."
"And what did they say?"
"They said they didn't know when they were going to respond to my email."

"Whose idea was it to move to Portugal?"
"Why are you not doing things in the way we are used to them being done? In England—"
"You said this would happen two weeks ago!"
"Did you see that link I sent you about—?"
"Do you think an 8 x 10m pool will be big enough?"
"Do you think we should do underfloor heating?"

"Well, do you remember the one we saw on (insert any one of the TV shows with House, Home, or any other derivative, in the title), that looked pretty cool, let's do something like that."

"Can we afford all this?"

Me: "HOW MUCH?"
(I think this may be a Yorkshire thing.)

There was a lot going on but some of the things that kept us going were; in the area we chose to build, people seemed happy and there had been a welcoming spirit alongside amazing help from local professionals, officials and business owners, there were decisions to make about which of the great value restaurants we would eat out at, each well-practised at serving a varied selection of grilled fish, but more importantly, there was the opportunity to start something new, a place to practice the alchemy for a good and happy life.

There was the opportunity to put faith in ourselves and each other and to see what we could do. The beach was also pretty close by. For us, Portugal was different, good different and when we were there, we were different, good different.

A fellow visitor, and subsequent resident of Portugal, who we'd met along our journey, suggested that the absence of express aisles in the supermarkets perhaps quintessentially explained Portugal's Algarve region. Why rush?

At this stage of our journey, we thought we were getting to grips with the Portuguese vibe (we didn't know how much we still needed to learn) and so, whenever we heard those Pips in the background with their "Things take time, this is Portugal," we just added our own, whoo! Whoo!

When Are We Moving to Portugal?

We had visions of making use of the regular flights and commuting backwards and forwards to Portugal and continuing our careers in the UK. We would each fly to and fro, on whichever day suited our schedule and try to maintain a professional presence in both countries.

We forgot to have the conversation about our carbon footprint and, to our shame, that conversation has still not been scheduled. We did make plans though. My wife is good, no scrap that, very good at making plans. Not just empty plans, mind you.

She had all the details, regardless of whether those details were actually in existence (I'm the same but for the purpose of appearing like I'm the sensible and measured one, we are not going to dwell on that).

So far, our detailed plan included my wife getting an ideal musical job, whether that be in an orchestra, international school, or both. The process began with the usual searching for opportunities and sending off CVs. It was no surprise when she got replies saying, "Yes, come for an audition and/or interview."

This probably had something to do with the fact that my wife has perfect pitch, is a professional violinist, pianist and oboist and has a wealth of experience in supporting and developing musical talent of all ages. Each offer was a legitimate reason to return to Portugal and I (solely for the purpose of moral support, of course), made sure I was available to accompany her.

We would fly in and my wife would have her audition/interview, during which, while embarking on a fact-finding mission enabling me to give a credible critique on the tourist experience of the Algarve, (a few beers here and there) I would maintain my supportive role.

In my head, the scenario would then play out as follows.

We would then go to the beach to await the news that she was being offered her ideal musical job. I would then be able to offer the aforementioned support and be on hand to celebrate.

Secretly, and perhaps now, not so secretly, I was ambivalent about her getting a job which meant she would be away from home for days or weeks on end. Would I have to make my own dinner? How exactly does the washing machine work? Would she forget about the domestic bliss we had created and planned to re-create in Portugal? Would she realise an ambition that had been hers since she was 10 years old that I wholeheartedly supported, but at best, would mean real changes for me?

Our post audition/interview trips to the beach became a reality; unfortunately, and I really do mean this, because the ideal job offer never came, I was able to avoid dealing with my own insecurities. I am, however, still working on those and luckily, my wife is helping!

The wonders of a particular internet search engine (other ones are available), led to my wife learning about a new international school. To cut a long story short, she contacted them and sent them her impressive CV. They agreed that she is fabulous and just what they were looking for and, like me, offered her a job.

Luckily for her, unlike the job I offered her (being my wife) their job paid well, had prospects and she could basically be her own boss. She accepted, and things again began to move at a pace. Then we bumped into those backing singers again, with their by now familiar and annoying chorus, "Things take time, this is Portugal."

We had to sell our house in England and plan the life changing move so the 'for sale' sign went up, we argued with the estate agent about why, because we had a nice house, we had to pay a percentage of the sale price, as opposed to the flat fee they charge for doing the same amount of work for a not so nice house and we told our families about our plans (by the way, we lost the argument with the devil, sorry, estate agent) and prepared for a quick sale of our fantastic house.

In the early planning stages (which we now realise were fuelled by enthusiasm, blind faith, and an oversized dose of naivety), we had planned that in a couple of months we would be in a position for building work to start. Within that time, because of the nature of mine and my wife's work, we would be available to meet with the relevant builders, tradesmen and officials, be on hand to celebrate the breaking of ground and continue to develop our dream of a new life.

As I've said, we are good at planning and had this plan all sorted, except of course for one small detail, Portugal basically closes in August. By that I mean everyone seems to go on holiday, either all at the same time, or one after another. Alongside that, we had not accounted for the Portuguese planning system which was, unsurprisingly, different from the English system.

The English planners gave you a rough timescale for when you should get your decision. In the event they failed to deliver, you could call them up and say, "I thought you said we'd have it by now!" This allowed you to feel you could influence the speed of the process.

The Portuguese system seemed to be, your plans go into the planners and you wait for their decision. That's it. You wait. No indication of timescale, or inkling of when you will hear back from them. Then when you do eventually hear, the plans must go back to the planners with the name of the specific builder who was doing your work.

To get a builder to agree to do your work, you have to first of all get some quotations, but many builders won't go to the trouble of doing a quotation until you have a construction licence (hear from the planners) and because you don't know when that might be, it is difficult to get accurate timescales get builders to schedule their workload and confirm their availability.

Meanwhile, the weeks flew by, the frustrations grew, the architect got sick of us asking for updates (while telling us because everything is urgent then nothing is urgent). Generally, the whole thing felt like a training programme for when you eventually lived there.

It's either you try and change the systems (while getting yourself wound up) or you keep hold of why you thought the prospect of eventually living in Portugal was a good idea in the first place and you purposely avoid the question, 'whose idea was this?'

So, we had one month waiting for the planners (which turned into 5 months) with nothing to do but wait. When I say nothing, I mean nothing. Neither of us were working, the house was looking fantastic in readiness for lots of prospective buyers and, because we were planning to build a house in Portugal and so needed to save money, we couldn't afford to go on holiday, or day trips.

The British summer weather was doing it's darndest to test the nation's flood defences, we had lots of TV channels and entertainment packages, DVDs, CDs, board games, etc. and we were bored. Sometimes we were frustrated, sometimes we were bored and frustrated, at times we were bored, frustrated and tetchy with each other all at the same time and then we were just bored again. Of course, we were making plans, with conversations like:

"Look at the weather, it won't be like this in Portugal."
"What are you most looking forward to when we move?"
"What are YOU most looking forward to when we move?"
"What would you like to do today, that doesn't cost any money?"
"What time is it now?"
"Let's go to another DIY store to look at the same things over again so we can start to plan, re-plan or revise what we are going to do when we start building."

"Let's watch another 'housey' programme about either; building a house, renovating a house, decorating a house, building a dream house, building a futuristic house, building a traditional house, making a traditional house into a modern house, designing a front room, a bedroom, a kitchen, building a dream house in Australia, New Zealand, somewhere in Europe, people relocating to another country, people buying a holiday home, planning a garden."

"OK."
"Wait a minute, we've seen this one before!"

We watched so many 'housey' programmes that we started to play a game in which we worked out whether we could remember the particular episode of a series just by reading the programme information guide. We could, so we stopped playing that game.

We both knew that every plan we made, talked about, revised and then talked about again was pointless, even though we had accounted for (made up) every detail that allowed us to believe our plan was a good one. We just had to wait.

One day, we looked at each other and it was obvious that neither of us wanted to say it, but we were bored. Then a bright idea (I think it was mine, but even if it wasn't, I'm claiming it).

"Let's get a cookbook and for every day this week, cook a different meal from a different region of the world."
"Excellent, an excuse to leave the house and do something, even if it was just going to the supermarket."

To be honest, it was a great success. We both really enjoyed it and the food was excellent. We still had no buyer for the house, no word from the planners or architect, and no word from most of the builders we had contacted. There was one last detail to add to our wait. I was told I was being made redundant.

Before the job that I was about to lose, I'd never really had a 'proper' job. Like my wife, I'd been a freelancer, working in the music industry as a performer and composer and in the education industry within Higher Education.

I enjoyed not being tied down to one job and thrived on the cut and thrust of self-employment and the ability to make each day different from the last. Then I was presented with an opportunity that offered a full-time contract and, perhaps more importantly a regular salary, in a role that at the time felt right.

A sense of stability, an opportunity to explore our dream of building a house and, for the first time, take regular holidays knowing that while we weren't working, we still had money coming in. The life of a freelancer, or self-employed couple, usually means holidays could be a costly business because both ends of the candle were being burnt. You were spending, but if you were not working, you were not earning.

Anyway, the feeling of this being a good opportunity proved to be true. It was something I enjoyed and proved to be good at. Unfortunately, in direct contrast to the benefits it gave us, the enjoyment faded and while I knew this wasn't a forever job for me, when I received that, 'you are going to be made redundant' phone call, I'm not sure what I thought first.

"How are we going to move to Portugal, build a house and live the dream?" We ARE going to move to Portugal, build a house and live the dream. "What will my wife say?"

I knew my plan making skills were working fine, but at that moment, I also knew I had almost zero confidence in my ability to provide the finer details as to how this particular plan, based on this new information, was going to be done.

My wife said, "It's a shock, we're a team and at least now we can move to Portugal without you pretending to your employers that you haven't moved to Portugal." (I'd been able to mostly work from home for the past year or so and, during idealistic date night conversations, for this to continue all I needed was a reliable internet connection).

For me, date nights were good for dreaming or romanticising about tomorrow, next week and the future. They were good for forming plans that made you think moving to Portugal was a great idea.

They were great for trying not to be too obvious (and in my case failing) about thinking your wife is looking fantastic and saying, "This is a great meal," while thinking, 'can we go home yet and when we get home, are you going to go to sleep straight away?' In our (or should I say my case), date nights were not so good for tackling the big questions in everyday life, such as:

"Can we afford this?"
"Will this really work?"

Buoyed by my wife's confidence, being made redundant wasn't necessarily the kybosh it, in the first instance, suggested it might be. In the '90s and noughties we had, like many, taken advantage of the UK property boom and had bought, renovated and flipped a few houses.

Yes we had made some money, but most of that had gone on the house we were currently living in that we couldn't afford when we bought it and were sick of not being able to afford now we were living in it.

Regardless of that, the main thing was as a result of our property development phase, I had an impressive array of tools, some newly found and subsequently developed skills and most importantly, a tool belt! Suffice to say the solution was obvious, I'd build the house of our dreams. Me and my tool belt.

After all, I could drink tea before starting work, I like a bacon sandwich and I'd done numerous jobs during our renovations that I had previously never tackled. How hard could it be? I could be the apprentice or labourer for a contractor and save money on the build. I could dust off my tool belt. Maybe even buy a new one?

Having a 'proper' job had its benefits and during the time of having it, I had developed new skills and competences that were attractive to other employers. I had also studied for and achieved a PhD. Many of my thoughts during what has become known as 'the tool belt phase', were perhaps ignited and subsequently fuelled by nights of good food, beverages and a supportive and indulgent wife who, as I had fun eyeing up particularly attractive tool belts, humoured me, but who ultimately encouraged me to see myself as she saw me.

To cut a long story short, I didn't buy a new tool belt, I got the mother of all drill sets, and a bigger and better job. The dream of building our Portuguese homestead (without me being involved in the actual building process) stayed alive.

My wife's new job started and the excitement that brought for her coincided with my own transition from one job to the next. It also brought with it the need for my wife to begin the process of a weekly commute to and from Portugal without me. Before this, I had been the one who went to and fro, while my wife's work had meant that she was largely based in and around where we lived.

Now, I had to come to terms with the fact that she was leading the charge, developing a wider professional profile. I had to stay at home with the added responsibility of looking after Marli, our cat (or should I say my wife's cat) who doesn't so much 'meow' but rather has a weird squeak, a thyroid condition and who sometimes appeared to have equal status in my wife's affections.

I had to play with her on a daily basis and think myself lucky that her litter tray was cleaned by my wife each week before she left. However, the main rule was 'under no circumstances was I to give Marli tuna. I think Marli agreed with Meatloaf, *2 out of 3 ain't bad!*

By this stage, we were both excited about the prospect of moving to Portugal and I was coming to terms with; waving my wife off each week (as she travelled to and from Portugal), excitedly waiting for her phone calls, and looking forward to the days when I could get in the car so I could go pick her up at the airport.

I felt immense pride in my wife's success and if I'm honest, lots of insecurities. It didn't help that me and Marli were left to our own devices, with no tuna.

Moving to Portugal

We received an acceptable offer for our UK home and set about putting our long held and over discussed date night plans into action. We excitedly began planning our road trip to get ourselves, Marli and a car over to Portugal. 1700 miles, an overloaded car and a cat that suffered from car sickness when going three miles to the vet. What could go wrong?

After all, we had our sunglasses, what else did we need? As the departure date approached, the anticipation grew and the topics of conversation were about what we could fit into a small car and whether Marli would be OK.

Finally, the eve of the big trip arrived. Car packed, a clink of glasses in celebration and early to bed for an early start in the morning. We had to drive to Folkestone, get the train across the channel and then, via France and Spain, make our way to Portugal. Simple.

The next morning was momentous to say the least. At the crack of dawn we sat in the car, we looked at each other, checked that Marli was safely in her cat basket and then looked at each other again.

> **Wife:** "We're doing it, we're really doing it."
> **Me:** "I can't believe it."

Wife: "Are you ready?"
Me: "Yes."
Me: "Are we doing the right thing?"
Wife: "Yes."
Me: "Marli, are you ready?"
Marli: "Squeak."
Me: "Then let's do this," and with that we started the car and began our journey.

Five minutes and a mile later.

Me: "Where's my wallet?"
Wife: "I don't know."
Me: "I think I've forgotten it."
Marli: "Squeak."
Me: "We better go back."

So, a great start to our momentous trip. It got even worse when we returned home, and the wallet was nowhere to be found.

Me: "It was here, have you moved it?"
Wife: "No."
Me: "You're always moving things, it was here, where is it, where have you put it?"
Wife: "I haven't moved it."
Me: "You must have done."
Wife: "I haven't moved it."
Marli: Squeak, very large yawn and then back to sleep.

So, before we had even properly set off, we were having the mother of all rows about the fact that I thought my wife was always moving things and the fact that my wife thought she didn't. This then escalated (as rows do), to the stuff we hang on to then, when it was least useful to do so, bring back. This was going to be a long road trip!

We found the wallet. It wasn't where I had last seen it. My wife did not move it and we'll say no more about it. Needless to say, the start (OK, second start) and first 10 or 20 miles of our momentous journey were done in stony silence as we both brooded and calmed down.

I liked driving and my old-fashioned values still got a kick out of romantic notions of a guy and his girl setting out on a road trip towards a new life (I'm sure there are better references but think Danny and Sandy in the closing scenes from Grease, 1978).

This meant, while my girl was across from me, looking great, I was looking forward to doing all the driving. Both things were achieved and the journey, approximately 1700 miles, taking in Northern France, inner city Paris, a ski resort, several toll roads, attempts to start games of I-Spy, service station offerings made into sandwiches (accompanied with our own pickled peppers packed specifically for this choice of menu), hotels sourced enroute and guy and gal games, it seemed as though my romantic notions were achieved. My notions, however, didn't know about the bridges.

It didn't occur to me that my fear of driving over bridges (which until now hadn't really been a big thing, but just one of those things we all have that we would rather not do), would be a major issue.

Unfortunately, my romantic notions failed to account for traversing vast expanses, the need for bridges, man's ability to construct in concert with natural phenomena, the geography of southern France, Northern Spain, the Pyrenees and finally Portugal, home to Europe's longest bridge and, showcasing engineering excellence in what seemed to be a study in road networks incorporating bridges, an impressive array of vast expanses negotiated by roads in the sky.

At times, it wasn't pretty. Sweaty palms and forehead, uncompromising, yet justified gestures of disapproval from drivers who didn't seem to care they, and we, were driving in the sky, my wife's well-meaning words of encouragement being heard as unhelpful help, responded to with choice language, which was driven by insecurity and, because I was grasping the steering wheel so tightly, an enormous ache in my shoulder.

My wife had never seen me have a 'thing' about a 'thing' before, something irrational that I found hard to cope with. This in itself was an additional something to deal with and slightly ruined what was my romantic notion. On the upside, Marli read her script, and was the perfect passenger, offering advice on when to make a rest stop, when a mealtime had been overlooked and on the quality of bed linen at our various hotels.

There was, of course, the prerequisite bridge from Spain to Portugal and while nervously uttering the words, "I think I'm gonna lose it," I drove across it. With the seeds of many a romantic story we arrived, a guy and his girl ready to start a new adventure.

We were lucky enough to secure a fully furnished apartment for rent that had a garden full of lemon and orange trees, an avocado tree and, complete with a rubber duck thermometer, a swimming pool. As the electric gates opened, and we drove up the gravel drive, for me, there was an overwhelming relief that we had arrived, without accident, acrimony, confusion or chaos.

We, including Marli, had survived our epic journey and we were greeted with the warm, beaming smile of our Yorkshire landlady. The people from Yorkshire had a reputation of being firm but fair, honest to the point of brutal and wary of strangers while being warm and friendly.

I knew I had parts 1, 2 and 3 of that heady mix and our landlady seemed to have the warm and friendly parts, so I immediately felt at home. There is something about human nature that makes you think because someone is from the same place as you there is more chance of having a meaningful connection with them.

That was not usually the case for me, as I'd met lots of Yorkshire folks to which I had taken an immediate dislike. If I haven't already mentioned, that is one of my faults and attributes, or perhaps Yorkshire traits.

I made snap judgements, which usually turned out to be correct (although that might be because I want them to be correct rather than they actually being correct); nonetheless, I usually make up my mind about a person very quickly, to which my wife usually says, "Give them a chance."

In an attempt to learn from my wife (something she will love reading when this is all over) and in an attempt to make Portugal a chance to reinvent myself, I tried desperately hard not to make a snap judgement about our landlady. I failed. I was me, making judgements upon judgements, for which I felt guilty but right about at the time.

Now I know I was guilty and wrong but, you can get the boy out of Yorkshire! Over the course of the following months, our landlady proved to be as warm and friendly as her initial greeting had suggested and within hours, she was inviting us to an evening out to one of her favourite restaurants.

Along with her partner, a Southerner from Southampton (but we won't hold that against him), they gave us the low down on their 20 something years of living in Portugal, the dos and don'ts, those who will and won't and lots of sound advice.

Landlady and partner 1, Yorkshire radar, nil.

The apartment was a modern two-bedroom annexe of the main house. Stylish, uncluttered, with a well-appointed living room with a kitchenette diner. The bedrooms were a good size, each with en-suite, heated floors and the kind of shower cubicle that welcomes you in and you resent leaving when you have finished.

I was particularly pleased that we wouldn't have to wrestle with shower curtains. We knew we had arrived at what could be considered our home for the next few months when Marli spread herself across the rug and then rolled over in anticipation of her first Portuguese tummy rub.

We had to keep remembering that we were not on holiday and although we were doing lots of holiday things; going to the beach, seeing the sights, eating out, enjoying the favourable prices of alcoholic beverages, we still had to make several trips back to Blighty.

We had to complete the sale of our house, arrange a removal firm and most of all, try to work out how we were going to fit the contents of our 5-bedroom house into our rented, fully furnished, two-bedroom apartment (more about that later).

We also had to remember we had to keep being patient with regards to the process of building our house. Being in Portugal made it harder to sit on our hands and do nothing. The temptation to just pop in to see the architect to ask, "Any news?" was hard to resist but, resist we did, because we knew the answer would be "NO!"

We also suspected that along with that no, there would be a desire, on our architect's part, to accompany that with, "How many times do I have to say, in Portugal you just have to wait." In reality, it was the same in England and we were well aware of the case studies we were used to reading in the numerous housey magazines, about self-builders and developers wrangling with planning authorities for months and sometimes years.

We were keen not to become one of those who, while enjoying all that Portugal had to offer, complained about the very infrastructure they decided to move to, so we took the view that while waiting for news of our planning application, we would try not to involve ourselves in the 'watched kettle syndrome.'

The weeks of waiting allowed for downtime, interspersed with regular flights back to England. We were both surprised at how quickly we had come to consider Portugal our home and whenever we flew back to England, standing on a train platform or waiting at a bus stop, in the midst of the commuter rat race, how quickly there was a feeling of being a visitor to England.

There was also the feeling that while among the commuters and amid the rat race, things seemed much more bearable because we were working on a master plan and (rightly or wrongly) we were able to make the assumption that those around us weren't.

The flights back also included chance meetings with interesting personalities. One such personality was a 40-something lady who, after spilling her bottle of red wine over me, proceeded to tell me about her impending divorce after a 22 year marriage (to a husband she no longer trusted and with whom she couldn't bear to be in the same house as), her boyfriend in Portugal who didn't quite understand her and her incontinent cat.

She had had an argument with her boyfriend before she boarded the plane and wanted my opinion on what she should do regarding her relationship with the boyfriend and what she should do with the rest of her life. My initial thought was, 'this was going to be a long flight'.

Surprisingly, and not for the first time since moving to Portugal, my Yorkshire radar let me down. It was probably one of the most enjoyable flights I've had, coming a close second to the flight that saw me being sat next to the CEO of a professional Rugby League Club with the rest of the team, full of international and world class players, being sat just a few rows down.

Being a massive rugby league fan, this was my opportunity to discuss all things rugby while giving my opinion on why the game wasn't more widely known, watched and respected amongst sport fans. The CEO in question was incredibly gracious, patient and told me he had enjoyed our conversation and that I had some interesting ideas that he wanted to follow up on. I am choosing to believe him.

The 40-something lady, who was keen to point out she was from the posh bit of Bradford, Yorkshire, and was now living in the posh bit between West and South Yorkshire, assumed that because I was a man, and her boyfriend was a man, I would immediately understand his point of view and therefore, be able to offer her sound advice, "well, you're a man, aren't you?"

When I reminded her, "not all men are the same," she didn't seem convinced so kept me thinking and chatting about relationships; relationships that develop, men who don't seem to be able to understand their wives or partners once a relationship has developed, men that don't listen, professional, experienced (and by now a bit tiddly) women like her who don't want to be tied to a traditional man with traditional views, whether she was in love with her Portuguese boyfriend or actually in love with Portugal, whether she should live in Portugal, Bradford, or Southampton (I thought I had a definite answer for that one).

Whether she should leave her marital home which, because she was excellent at it, she had expertly decorated, whether she should go back into working in HR or pursue a career in interior design and a few other things that seemed important to her at the time, but surprisingly unimportant to me right now.

By the time we landed, I had of course; considered and addressed all the issues, formulated a specific and personal life plan for her and, much to her frustration and probable annoyance, until we were at the baggage carousel and were about to go our separate ways, I had avoided telling her anything about me. "I'm Paul, it's been nice to meet you."

The weeks of waiting were also a time when, during quiet times, long walks, car journeys with the top down, shopping trips, getting sand between our toes (and everywhere else) and generally feeling a sense of pride in our bravery, we often exchanged knowing glances to each other followed by conversations that made us realise that, in moving to Portugal, we had done the right thing, with perhaps the only mistake being we hadn't done it sooner. There was also another revelation, life's better with your sunglasses on.

It was then time to return to England to do the last bits of packing and complete the sale of our house. The process of selling it had moved quite quickly at first, with an offer in the first few weeks. Then, perhaps ironically, there were delays that seemed to develop from nowhere and to which no-one had the answer as to when they were going to be resolved.

Perhaps our backing singers, as we took our trip to England, had stowed away in our cases, intent on reminding us, "Things take time in England too, Whoo Whoo!"

We (it was really just me), had toyed with the idea of driving a removal van ourselves, from Blighty to Portugal laden with all our worldly possessions.

"It'll be fun, we'll have a laugh and it will save us a lot of money," **I said.**
"Hmm! I'm not so sure," **wife said.**
"Let's work it out, to see if it will save us some money," **wife said.**
"It'll be fun, we'll have a laugh," **I said.**
"We can pretend to be proper truckers, eat cooked breakfasts along the way, and you can ride shotgun," **I said.**
"We should get a proper firm to do it," **wife said.**

"It'll be a laugh; how hard can it be?" **I said.**

"Just imagine. You and me. On the open road. The highway to our new life with all our worldly possessions," **I said.**

"We should get a proper firm to do it," **wife said.**

We got a proper firm to do it. Well, nearly.

Early quotes came in at thousands and, with my trusty Yorkshire traits, I was not that keen on speeding money. So of course, there had to be a cheaper way. There was. Did we use the cheaper way? Yes, we did. Would we do it again? No, we would not.

Adopting the tried and tested method of typing something into a search engine so that all your questions could be answered and problems solved, the solution I arranged (and my wife agreed to) involved some very Heath Robinson type calculations as to the volume of stuff we wanted to move, its weight (in relation to haulage regulations), a requirement to leave the house we were selling by 2pm (even though we had no idea what time the vehicles would arrive) and two Polish van drivers.

So far, arrangements had gone according to plan, so much so that within a couple of days, the price was right, they had a list of our belongings, they had advised us that we really needed two vehicles (not just the one I had initially suggested) and assured us that everything, including our baby grand piano, was in safe hands.

What they failed to point out was that the drivers would not be from the same company; neither spoke English (we don't speak Polish), they would be coming from two separate destinations in Poland at different times, that each had a different return schedule and therefore, would not arrive in Portugal at the same time or (and this was likely) potentially not on the same day.

Wrapped up in all of this was the added worry of 'What if this firm are a band of cowboys who, after we help load all of our possessions into their vans, ride off into the sunset, never to be seen again?' We had left it too late to organise anything with anyone else, so we made an executive decision. We went with the 'well, we're insured, aren't we?' approach.

Moving day arrived and, as we waited, expectantly, eagerly and excitedly for our crack team of removers to arrive, introduce themselves and fly into action, there was the rumble of heavy goods vehicles. With a sigh of relief I thought great, the firm had arrived as promised and I went to introduce myself to the driver.

The driver looked as you would perhaps expect, or at least fitted my stereotypical notion of what a removal man looked like. A proper trucker who obviously ate cooked breakfasts, probably wasn't a vegan or teetotaller, was as confident, brash and bullish as he was round and had a partner riding shotgun that looked like a partner in crime who also did some removals on the side.

It was only when they introduced themselves did we realise they were the firm for the people who were moving into our house. They had arrived early in order to 'get cracking' and were wondering when we would be finished and out by.

The look on his face when I said, "Oh, our removers aren't here yet, we don't know what time they will arrive and we haven't even started getting our things out of the house yet," suggested that firstly, our futures were probably going to be much more pleasant if we never saw each other again and secondly, this was going to be a busy day.

Me telling them our drivers were Polish and charged considerably less than they, in hindsight, probably was never going to be what they wanted to hear. I think it was fair to say we didn't warm to each other and relations were set to get damn right frosty.

Then, in a blaze of glory, our crack team of two drivers arrived. They had never met each other, it was questionable whether one of them had had a meal, never mind a cooked breakfast, and they didn't seem all that bothered that by now we only had four hours to clear the house.

On the flip side, one of our drivers did have a snazzy little tap thing on the underside of his van so he could wash his hands whenever he wanted. I thought that was pretty cool. What we also noticed was that neither of them had the correct equipment for moving a baby grand piano. We thought that was very uncool.

It quickly became apparent that our drivers had very few details about our job. They had not been given the list of our belongings and they didn't know about our hot tub, American style fridge freezer, 3 piece suite, cross trainer, 3 drum kits, 24 violins, 1 cello, 10 chairs (one of which was an old style rocking chair), my new power tools, the things people acquire in life, the things people buy in life, the things (because they were overlooked) we didn't mention to the removal firm and, surprise surprise, something we certainly did mention, our baby grand piano.

Polish driver 1: "You have a piano?"

Cue much Polish chatter between our two removal protagonists. Human behaviour often has an innate ability to transcend any barriers of language and, despite our lack of Polish speaking skills, it was clear that whatever it was they were saying to each other, it wasn't good.

Polish driver 2: "This is very heavy."

We, of course, already knew these two key bits of information. It was just a shame that firstly, our drivers didn't and secondly, the other firm could hear our animated and Google Translate enhanced conversations. They could tell things weren't necessarily going to plan and I suspect they took some delight in asking, "Exactly how much are these guys charging you?"

Me: "Less than you would have done."

That was the first time me and them had been in agreement since we'd met. It was also the last. We began loading our pre-packed boxes into our first vehicle in the knowledge that we had approximately 3 hours to load everything we owned before we were officially supposed to hand over the keys to the new owners.

We thought we were well prepared but there is always more stuff that you imagine and stuff you don't even remember buying, owning, using, wanting anymore, or stuff you can't really see a future use for. That said, everything had to go.

So there I was, going back and forth from garage to vehicle and back again, while my wife did her level best to keep calm, clean the house from top to bottom and not overly worry about the fact that, with an hour to go, we were nowhere near finished.

To make matters worse, the new owners turned up early with the question, "do you know when you'll be finished? We have the children with us, and they are getting restless." Why is it that people with children think that they deserve some special consideration based on the fact that they have children?

Yes, we were running late and yes, our crack team of removal men weren't quite so crack, but did they think we were going to go faster because they had children? We were going as fast as we could. If I'm honest, and I'm not proud of it, I actually got some enjoyment from causing them a little bit of inconvenience and I suspect my wife did too.

They had been difficult during the selling and buying phase and, as we saw it, because of them, we were moving two months later than we had originally planned, so from our point of view, they and their children could wait.

It was then time to load the piano. Luckily, I had a set of wheels handy. The same set of wheels my wife had been trying, for the past few years, to get me to throw out. The joy of being able to say, "I told you they would come in handy," was more fun than it should have been and I was determined to enjoy every minute of it.

What I didn't enjoy was the real possibility of ruining our beloved baby grand. There was much huffing, puffing, effing and jeffing, as the other removal firm looked on, while my wife worried about my back because of the lifting, the piano (that now had a massive chunk out of it), the door frame (that now had a massive chunk out of it), the step we nearly forgot about and whether, along with the piano and everything else, would we get the 8 foot yucca plant in as well.

My wife had bought me the yucca as a housewarming present when I bought my first house, some 24 years previous and had become a bit of a symbol of our relationship. It just had to fit in.

Our 2pm deadline came and went, the new owners got annoyed, the other removal crew became very annoyed, then aggressive, then petulant, more red faced, further annoyed and even more red-faced. I wanted to laugh a little, immature I know, but the naughty boy in me is rarely that far away from the surface.

My wife, because she was fully aware of my naughty boy abilities, gave me a look that told me she knew I wanted to laugh. I suspect she also could have had a giggle. Anyway, we managed to stifle our naughtiness, my wife was proud of me and we had a knowing smile between us.

Finally, two hours late with one removal crew thoroughly annoyed and delayed, one set of new owners thoroughly annoyed and delayed, some restless children, inconvenienced neighbours (because of all the vehicles), two overloaded vans each with a Polish driver at the wheel, yucca and all, we were loaded and ready to enact one of my romantic visions.

As we watched the vans drive away towards our new life, my wife and I had a hug, a kiss, another hug and a bit of a longer hug. We had done it. Sold it, packed it, and fitted it all in.

As we drove away, we both had knowing smiles. We were doing the right thing. We also had in our minds, we hope we see our stuff again.

We Live in Portugal

No sooner had we waved our belongings off, with the ringing of the annoyed still in our ears, it was time to welcome it back at our new home in the Algarve. As we patiently (OK, not so patiently) waited for our Polish drivers to call with an ETA, all thoughts of never seeing our belongings again had gone, well nearly gone.

Cue massive sigh of relief when the phone went, and Polish driver number 1 told us he'd be with us in the next hour. Now, we just had to wait for Polish driver number 2. True to his word, Polish driver number 1 arrived. He had been driving for 3 days and looked like he'd been driving for a week.

He was wearing the same clothes as 3 days ago, complete with a funny little woollen hat and he was as prickly as he had been when he left us in England. When we inquired about the whereabouts of driver number 2, it became clear that they were not together and had not travelled together.

Driver number 1 had no idea about driver number 2 and didn't know when we could expect him. Driver number 1 also wasn't in the mood to phone driver number 2 on our behalf. So, with pleasantries ignored, we began the task of unloading the first vehicle.

In all honesty, the unloading went quite well, and we quickly developed a routine of Polish driver number 1 to me, me to my wife and my wife to anywhere with a space. As we carefully inspected each item, we were relieved to discover nothing was broken, or damaged and, at times, there was even the faintest glimmer of a smile on the face of Polish driver number 1.

Then we found out that back in Poland, he was a musician and much to our amazement, we even found time for a pleasant chat about him, his wife, his music, etc. My Yorkshire radar had seen the grumpy side of him but it either missed this side of him or this side of him was previously in stealth mode.

Either way, as we unloaded the final few pieces, it became clear that driver number 1 had been cajoled into taking this job, had not been given the right information, was due to be very badly paid and wanted to get home to his family.

All things being considered, it was perhaps understandable that he wasn't the life and soul of our removal party. After all the unpacking, as he drove away, we did eventually get to see him smile.

Our two-bedroom apartment had managed to house all the contents of van 1, while at the same time, our two-bedroom apartment looked like it was never going to house all the contents of van 1. We still had no idea when van 2 would arrive but what we did know was, it was going to be a tight squeeze.

The following morning, we woke to one of the worst storms in recent Portuguese history, with torrential rain and wind. We also woke to the sound of our telephone, with Polish driver number 2 proudly telling us he was outside and ready to start unloading. So we had moved to a country with approximately 300 days sunshine a year yet, on the day we want to unload a van of our belongings, including the baby grand piano, the settees, beds, mattresses, cushions (why so many cushions?) and all the other types of soft furnishings and things that soaked up water, it was lashing down.

Driver number 2 was much younger than driver number 1 and a much quieter personality. He too had been given only half of the details for our job and it was easy to tell that he too wasn't necessarily having the best of times. He looked fresher faced than driver number 1 but decidedly more wet and, as the wind and rain appeared to wait for us to start unloading before really getting going, it was clear that on this day, there were no good times to be had by any of us.

Driver number 2 was a hard worker and dutifully helped with the unloading as he and I went back and forth across the gravel drive. There was an attempt to try and keep things dry. We failed. Everything got soaked. The contents of van number 2, added to the contents of van number 1 were now beginning to address the question, 'can you fit 12 years in a 5-bedroom house into a two-bedroom apartment?'

While we looked for an answer to that question, the grand piano was still to be moved from the van to its temporary resting place. As the Portuguese rain continued in biblical proportions, our two-bedroom apartment was beginning to fill up with our increasingly soggy belongings. The question of whether we could fit everything in was being answered as a new question arose, can we fit everything in and still leave room for us?

Everything was everywhere and rather than finding a permanent home for everything, the rain meant that our main focus was on just getting everything in. Then it was time for the piano. The gravel drive meant that my trusty set of wheels were struggling to ease the passage from van to apartment and so it was left to brute force.

Cue huffing and puffing, several swear words, a trapped finger, a worried wife, a scare that we had damaged our rental property's door frame, a Polish driver who didn't sign up for this and another couple of scratches. Eventually, with one last shove, the piano was in. We'd done it. We'd moved to Portugal and, as we waved off Polish driver number 2, we were left shattered, cramped, soggy and very relieved.

Wife: "Shall we go for a drink?"
Me: "I think we deserve more than one!"
Marli: "Squeak!"

We Really Live in Portugal

When we decided we were going to move to Portugal, it seemed like a gargantuan undertaking. How were we going to do this? As well as all of the other things you don't think about when you decide to move abroad, the things like international driving licences, utility companies, bank accounts and basically all of the 'little' things my wife deals with on a weekly, monthly, annual basis that I either take for granted, or get done by magic fairies, we also had to sell the house, move jobs (in my case find a job), get Marli settled, drive the car over and find a place to rent.

Now we were actually living in Portugal, it was surprising just how quickly all that was forgotten and it immediately felt like we had just decided to move and then, with the help of the magic fairies, had just gone ahead and done it.

So we could show our friends and families back home just what a wonderful thing we had done, we both made sure we made time for 'a view from the office window' type photographs. The kind of thing you send just to make sure everyone knows you're basking in sunshine or at the beach or a seafront restaurant, complete with beverage and a smug grin on your face.

For me, these got a bit tiring but for my wife, well. We did a brave thing and I think my wife just wanted people to know we did a brave thing, so her camera, and her knowledge of the comparative temperatures of the Algarve and West Yorkshire got more use than mine.

We quickly got used to picking citrus fruit from the various trees in our rented garden, not starting each morning conversation with, "what's the weather like?" Having the top down on the car, calculating how much less everything was costing, discussing all the bad things about England and why Portugal was so much better.

Admittedly, I suspect some of these discussions were illuminated by the rose-tinted glare our sunglasses gave us as we walked hand in hand along the various beaches that were only minutes away.

We were also getting used to the different ways in which the Portuguese seemed to do things. When I say getting used to, you could say we were getting used to being frustrated at the way the Portuguese seemed to do things. When discussing this with fellow Brits, it seemed the biggest frustration was Portuguese bureaucracy and the lack of a specific timetable on when you could get that piece of paper, and in some cases where you should go to get the necessary bit of paper that allowed you to get the next bit of paper.

In Portugal, to get anything done, you need a stack of official documents for everything. It's probably the same everywhere, yes even England, but perhaps the fact that the Portuguese seem to start work somewhere between 9am and 10am (in the case of our lawyer approximately 11am, although that's not guaranteed), have strictly legislated and what seemed like relaxed extended lunch breaks that were enjoyed and taken by everybody at the same time (there's even a daily siren for the whole town telling people it's time for lunch), wear casual clothing (complete with trainers) even for office based jobs, don't feel the need to acknowledge receipt of emails (so you are never quite sure if something has been received and is being acted on) and generally seemed very relaxed, gives us Brits the feeling that things take too long over here.

My wife had made the observation that the Portuguese never quite gave you the whole story, reminiscent of the comedy gag, 'Does your dog bite?' In case you don't know the joke, on seeing a man beside a dog, our protagonist asks the man if his dog bites.

"No," replies the man, so our protagonist bends to stroke the dog and is duly bitten.

"You said your dog doesn't bite," yells our protagonist.

"That is not my dog," the man says.

Similarly, getting used to life in Portugal at times felt like you had to know which question to ask, even though you don't always know you need, or would need, to ask that question. We realised that, for our own sanity, we had to find a balance between here, where we wanted to be and there, where we didn't want to be.

We also had to keep reminding ourselves why we were drawn to Portugal in the first place and keep a balanced perspective, otherwise, we would drive ourselves into the ground with frustration. We didn't always manage to keep a balance, but on the flipside, when things got a bit too much, we were able to continue our balancing capers down by the beach, where, after a day of Anglo-Portuguese frustrations, things just seemed better.

Perhaps unsurprisingly then, in our first few months of living in Portugal, we saw a lot of the beach. While we were waiting and waiting and waiting for our nirvana to begin rising from the Portuguese hillsides, the opportunity came up to buy some land directly across the road. This was also the opportunity to resume our heated debate.

Me: "Pigs." (Nothing to discuss really, we're having two.)
Wife: "Goats."
Me: "Not before I get my pigs."
Wife: "Goats."
Marli: "Shh!"
Either: "Chickens?"
Wife: "Goats are good for clearing the land and will help prevent fire. Read one of several email links, council leaflets, Facebook posts, informational films, WhatsApp chats, Instagram posts, tweets, etc. that I am going to bombard you with. You'll know which ones they are they'll be the ones after the posts about llamas and alpacas!"
Me: "If you're looking after all those animals, when will you have time to look after me?"
Wife: "Muffled sounds—something something—off!"

As you can see, I didn't quite catch her response. Nonetheless, after she said whatever she said, two things were very clear. Firstly, this was going to be one of the few times when my devastatingly handsome smile cut no ice and secondly, it was also one of the frequent times when I knew the conversation wasn't over.

While we were still waiting and waiting and waiting for our nirvana to begin rising from the Portuguese hillsides, I was doing the weekly commute from Portugal to England. When we were planning this new adventure, the idea of me flying back and forth seemed completely simple, feasible and not that much of a first world hardship.

The idea also rested on me doing a job I liked, in a place I liked, with people I liked. On top of that, the idea didn't account for my wife's tales of beach trips without me, my feelings of not being in control of everything, not being there (in the event of a crisis), equally frightened and, on one occasion after just landing back in England, a panicked phone call.

Me: "Hi, I've just landed." (I could tell she was driving and thought, what's she doing out this late?)
Wife: "Marli's really ill and I'm taking her to the emergency vet, I'm really worried about her and I can't talk right now because I need the phone for sat nav. I'll call you later."

The idea of me commuting to and from Portugal had a major flaw in it. It meant that I had to come to terms with my newly confident and blossoming wife and the fact that I may not always be able to be there to take control, (whether that is what is required or not) offer support, a shoulder to cry on, or a tension easing witty aside (well, I think they're witty).

When the phone went again, about 20 minutes later, I didn't like the sound of fear and panic in my wife's voice and even more so, I didn't like my feelings of helplessness and knowing my wife was on her own. I also wanted to see Marli.

Wife: "She's had some scans."
Me: "Are you ok?"
Wife: "She's had some scans."
Me: "But are YOU ok?"
Wife: "Yes, she's had some scans and they say for a cat her age, 17, she's in good health and has a slight infection that can be cleared up with some tablets. The vet only cost 49 euros; it would never be that in England."
Me: Huge sigh of relief (about Marli and the vet's bill).

I now knew things were going to be OK, my wife's panic was over, and I was going to get the chance to rub Marli's tummy again. I also now knew that vet bills in Portugal were cheaper than they were in England. I also knew I didn't want to be commuting for much longer.

Things Get Going in Portugal. Oh No They Don't. Well, just a Little Bit

As we waited for updates about our building project, in the news both in England and Portugal, the terms Corona Virus and Covid-19 were beginning to be mentioned on a daily basis. At first, it was something that was happening somewhere else in the world and it somehow felt although we should be aware of it, it was never going to be something we would ever have to actually deal with.

Then suddenly, almost overnight, it was here, everywhere, very serious and something for everyone to deal with. My wife's school was already mentioning 'going into lockdown' and although we knew what the term meant, we didn't REALLY know what it meant for us and the rest of the world. We were soon to find out.

I was in England, planning and scheming just how I was going to end the commuting, while my wife and Marli were in Portugal, where this Corona/Covid thing was being talked about with much more urgency and seriousness, then my phone rang.

Wife: "It's official, the whole country is going into lockdown, my school is shutting, I have to work from home. What is the news in England? Maybe they will shut England down and you can work from home, your new home of Portugal!"

Me: "I think that's just wishful thinking, so let's not even think about it. It would be too good to be true. I'll see you on the weekend."

The weekend came, I landed in Portugal for my usual weekend visit and I got to spend time with my wife, rub Marli's tummy (several times) and continue scheming and planning our building project and how I was going to engineer a way of staying in Portugal. As usual, no sooner had I arrived it was time to get back on a plane and return to England, except this time was different.

As I landed back in Blighty, I got the news. England was going into lockdown and everyone had to work from home. Within an hour of landing, I had booked a return flight and within 24 hours, I was home. Me, my wife and Marli. Just how we liked it.

Me: "Now that I'm here, we can really drive this project forward. We can be on our architect's case much more and hurry things along."

Wife: "Yes, it will be easier to show a united front."

Marli: "I'm sick of hearing about this bloomin' house they are building. Isn't it time I had another tummy rub?"

We should really have known to take whatever our architect said with a large dose of salt, after all, she told us we would be able to start our build in 6 months. That was 12 months ago, and we still hadn't started. For some reason, despite our experiences so far, we were still naive enough to think, just because we were both in Portugal, our architect would suddenly burst into life.

Well, as I'm sure you can guess, there was no bursting into anything or anywhere and, as we got increasingly frustrated with the slow progress, the final straw came.

Portugal is famous for many things and proud of them all. One such thing is cork and the trees on which it grows. Portugal is so proud of its cork trees that if, without permission, you cut one down, you get a hefty fine and you could be banned from using or building on your land for 25 years.

Our land had several cork trees on it and our architect, who we thought might be aware of such stringent rules, had designed us a house which relied on the trees being chopped down. Additionally, when our architect told us, "the cork trees, oh yes, they won't be a problem," we thought she meant, the cork trees wouldn't be a problem. What she actually meant was, "Oh yes, the cork trees, that's going to be a problem, you better get up there quickly and chop them down."

Me and Wife: "But what about the law that says blah blah blah, hefty fine, 25 years etc.?"

Architect: "Ah, yes."

Me and Wife: "Why didn't you tell us about this?"

Architect: "You didn't ask."

Me and Wife: (Incredulous looks, fury, rage, swear words under our breath, although some nearly popped out, and a desperate attempt not to leap across the desk of our ill-informed, slow and now perilously close to physical harm architect.)

Me: (Unable to talk)

Wife: "Well, can we apply to have them chopped down?"

Architect: "Yes."

Wife: "How do we go about doing that?"

Me: (Still unable to talk, as I desperately try to remember everything my mother told me about being nice to people.)

Architect: "We must fill in a form and submit that to the council."

Wife: "How long will that take?"

Architect: "I don't know."

Wife: "Do you have the form?"

Architect: "No. I must get it from the council."

Me: (In my head) 'Well go and get the £&*%^£ form right now, you £$%*&^, annoying—'

Wife: "Well, can you do that please and we will fill it in."

After a few days, the form was presented to us and we filled it in and, safe in the knowledge we had at last applied to have the cork trees removed, we handed it to our architect. Fast forward a couple of weeks and we receive an official looking document from ICNF (Instituto da Conservacao da Natureza e das Florestas), basically the body that looks after the conservation and flora of Portugal.

What our architect didn't tell us (and after being in Portugal for a while now, you could say we should have known better) with all official processes in Portugal, it was never as simple as it could be and moreover, it seemed like it was someone's job to make things as convoluted as possible.

It turned out, what our architect had presented us with was an application form that would grant us permission to make an application to get permission. Yes, Portugal struck again. We needed permission to ask for permission. The document from the INCF was an 18-point list of things we needed to supply or comply with in order to begin the process of actually applying to have the cork trees removed.

We received this document just as we had finished lunch and with words such as, 'straw', 'camel' and 'that bloody, bleep, bleep, architect' coming to mind, our conversation went something like this.

Me: "I'm not sure we should continue working with this architect."

Wife: "I know what you mean but is it better the devil you know?"

Marli: (He looks really angry; I hope he doesn't know that while they were out, I was climbing all over the kitchen table).

Me: "At this rate, we'll go bonkers with the stress of it. I'm sick of it. We need a new architect."

Wife: "Will we have to start again?"

Marli: (I know! If I use my collapsible legs trick and roll over for a tummy rub, they'll not notice the fur on the table).

Me: "I don't care, I can't go on like this." (Cue the sound of fingers tapping on my keyboard, G>O>O>G>L>E and then A>R>C>H>I>T>E>C>T>S space N>E>A>R> space M>E.)

Wife: "Ah! Look at Marli, she wants a tummy rub. Who's a beautiful girl?"

Marli: (Never fails!)

Google came through for us and, in no time at all, we had sacked the original architect and we had found ourselves a new and improved version. In hindsight, it was probably the best thing (apart from the money we had already paid to the first one).

When starting this, 'building a house in Portugal', journey we were living in England and so we had set about trying to create a house like the one we had. The difference was, as we were now realising, we needed a house for people who actually lived in Portugal, not for people who want to live in Portugal but without the howling wind, rain, and Yorkshire charm of Slaithwaite, or a house for people who wanted to show their English friends and family just how successful they had been in being able to build a massive house abroad.

Our English house was big, too big for us three and in reality, there were rooms we didn't use, need, or even go in that often, so why were we trying to re-create what we had, when the purpose of moving in the first place was to downsize a little and live a simpler life?

So, the process of designing a house for people who lived in Portugal began and the results were beginning to look totally different and very much more exciting. Our new architect also smashed some of the myths we had been told about Portuguese people.

We were told the Portuguese were not very good at responding to emails and so when our first architect was a poster child for that, we put it down to them being laid back and Portuguese and us being English and uptight. It turned out people are people and they could be more reliably characterised by type than nationality.

Who knew? The new architect was great at responding to our questions, emails, sent us drawings within days, emails on Sunday evenings and almost blasted the stereotype out of the water. I say almost. Bearing in mind we didn't always know what questions needed to be asked, sometimes more, or auxiliary information, would have been useful.

So, all in all, while the world was coping, or at least getting used to life with Corona Virus and Covid 19 and bearing in mind I don't really like people, or going out, or having to accept invitations to events I don't really want to go to, or see people I don't miss seeing, or going to restaurants where the food is not better than we cook at home, or result in my wife being ill because of her dietary requirements and service staff who don't listen or take it seriously and, because I can be just a bit mardy (Yorkshire for grumpy), lockdown was working quite well for us.

We had found a new architect, who was moving things forward at a pace, we didn't have to see or be with anybody and the 3 of us were able to be together. If only we could start the build.

While we waited for our new improved architect to finish the plans for our new improved house, we got used to living in Portugal. We also decided that while we were waiting, we had ½ an acre of land sitting there doing nothing. Can't quite remember whose idea it was (so I'm taking the credit).

Me: "Shall we start a little garden up there? We could just dig over a patch, make a few raised beds and start growing some vegetables. What do you think?"

Wife: "Oh, that is a great idea, you are so clever."

OK, I might have exaggerated the last bit of her response there but, to cut a long story short, we started a vegetable patch with 3 raised beds, some seeds and our wellies which, when paired with a pair of shorts, looked particularly good on my wife. My shorts just kept slipping down every time I bent over.

We were doing something on our land, and it felt great. I had my trusty shovel and I was able to direct operations, what more could a man ask for? I know, a wife who actually listened to said directions!

It was while gardening, one in shorts looking great and one not so much, that the idea of maybe starting to do more than just this bit of gardening first took hold.

I'm not sure who thought of it but, to avoid confusion, let's just say it was me,. This next conversation is quoted verbatim (for 'verbatim' read 'sort of').

Me: "Why don't we do more than this bit of gardening?"
Wife: "Oh, that is a great idea, once again, you are so clever, I'm so lucky to be married to someone so wonderful and inventive."
Me: "Yes, you are, dear."
Wife: "My hero!"

(Cue dramatic music, wide angle lens shot of a loving couple in a field and—) Well, I think you get the drift.

We knew where on our land we wanted our house to be built and so we knew where we could start doing some work without it affecting the eventual build. Moreover, we were just desperate to start doing something useful and to feel like we were making progress.

I was also desperate for a legitimate reason to go shopping, a reason to get a tool belt and perhaps more importantly, a chance to use my new power tools, DEWALT-TASTIC! (Other manufacturers are available.)

So, we identified an area where we could start to plan our very own garden (with some extra bits) on our Portuguese land for our Portuguese house. Exciting!

In reality, because the land was so overgrown, beginning work was really moving earth and stones from point A to point B, then changing our minds and realising that some of the earth that was originally at point A should have stayed there, so we had to move it back again.

Along with the times when me directing operations was not, well, let's just say 'appreciated', there were several times when we wished we had considered points C, D and E. Within that though we did get several shopping trips in and during one such trip, we bought a 'Carro de Mao' (wheelbarrow), a bright green one that was 33 euros.

At the time of purchase, I couldn't understand why some carro de maos were priced at 91 euros when they all looked pretty similar to me. Why would anyone pay 91 euros when they could pay 33? Therefore, true to my Yorkshire heritage and frugality, I chose the bright green one.

It wasn't until I started to mix cement in it, and all of the paint started to come off into the cement, that I realised why someone would pay 91 euros for a carro de mao. We also bought our very own van, a blue van that, in honour of my rugby watching electrician friend back in England, we named 'Dave'.

Let's face it, every building team needed their own van, I mean, you couldn't be a building outfit if you hadn't got your own van. So, there we were, foreman and builders' mate, riding along, tools at the ready, and fire in our bellies (although to be a proper English building team that should have been bacon butties), turning up for work on our own building site to work on our own and brand-new garden.

It felt great. The starting of works was also an opportunity to start tracking our progress towards our new house. With this in mind, we began taking pictures showing the before, during and after stages of our hard labour. Seeing what's been done, the progress and knowing that you've done it, was a great motivator and although, due to the blazing sunshine, the digging was hard.

Remembering Noel Coward's well-known ditty about 'Mad Dogs and Englishmen,' we often started at 7am, but we loved every minute of it; the sweating (resulting in draining our wellies and wringing out socks), seeing the bubble on the spirit level go from.

Me: "That's well off."

to

Wife: "Bang on!"

needing to buy a new pair of gloves because the first pair had worn out, the joys of listening to the inventive excuses my wife made up as to why she couldn't possibly lift another stone, the bottles of 'Super Bock' (one of the local beverages) that punctuated every little victory or signalled the end of another days work.

More than all these though, we were doing what had been discussed on all those date nights, late nights, early mornings and everything in between. We were actually doing it! I still needed a tool belt, but now, the big issue to consider was what colour belt would go with our new van.

Before we left to start our new life in Portugal, one of our concerns was whether, or how, Marli would cope with the over 300 days of glorious sunshine. When in England, the slightest bit of sunshine resulted in her finding the exact spot where the sun shone through on to the carpet or rug and then dramatically stretching out.

When she did this, my wife said she reminded her of Cleopatra, as she ordered her slaves to peel her another grape. For me, it was more like one of those furry draft excluders you put under your door. Either way, we both agreed that she liked the sunshine, but would she cope with the sunshine and the heat?

Well, in the time we had spent so far, she seemed to revel in it and, to our surprise, apart from the one episode of illness, she seemed to be taking to Portugal, as were we, like a duck to water (or should that be like a cat to tuna? Oops, don't mention tuna!) Anyway, apart from the occasional hair ball, she was loving it, we were loving it and things couldn't be better.

Then I noticed rather than the usual.

Me: "She'll be fine."
Me: "You spoil her."
Wife: "She's my baby."
Marli: (Mummy, are you sure we need him?)
Me: "She's just a cat. Stop fussing over her. Marli, GET OFF THE TABLE!"

Something wasn't quite right. I'd always thought of Marli as my wife's cat and I'm pretty sure Marli just thought of me as a necessary evil and the person who, from time to time, occupied her perfect spot for cuddles with mummy. That being said, I must admit we had our moments together and I noticed that in recent weeks, there had been no Marli-daddy moments.

Then one night as my wife (who goes to bed too early for my liking, but that's probably a whole different conversation) was in bed and I watched my usual American cops and robber's TV show, there was something definitely not right. There were occasions when I didn't pay Marli much notice, but this night was not one of them.

It was clear she was uncomfortable and distressed and, when I saw a spot of blood, it also became clear that I had to do something. So, like every good superhero, I woke my wife. I was just pleased (and quite frankly proud of myself) that I had firstly, noticed something and, more importantly, I was there to support my wife as the inevitable worry and panic started to creep up.

Wife: "I'm phoning the vet."

Me: (*Thinking it but not daring to say it.*) "How much is that going to cost?"

Vet: "Bring her in in the morning."

Wife: (Look of sheer fright and panic.)

Me: (There is no way my wife will be able to watch her like this until the morning.)

Marli: (Cry of pain).

Me: (*Wait a minute, she never makes sounds like that.*) "Get dressed, we are taking her to the vet NOW!"

I had always known that there would be a day when three of us go and two of us return. I'd always known that when that day arrived, I would not have a clue how to deal with my wife's grief and I knew that my natural instinct would be to ask the vet for a cheaper option, which bearing in mind the situation, would probably be just one of the many wrong things that I would say.

What I didn't know was whether that day had arrived. As we drove to the vet, with Marli making sounds I'd never heard and didn't like, my wife tried to calm her down. I knew this was as much for her own benefit as for Marli's, but she was adopting the kind of tone that cat lovers used when speaking to their cats. I didn't understand that tone of voice and, to be honest, I found it quite annoying, but I thought it best not to discuss it at that moment.

When we arrived at the vets, our panic levels were boiling over, my wife's for some of the right reasons, mine for some of the wrong ones. When I was metaphorically compiling my list of 'things not to say', I didn't realise that on that list should have been 'don't even mention the possibility of our car journey home having one less occupant'. My oversight was pointed out (in very clear terms) and a new draft of the list was quickly compiled.

Vet: "How old is your cat?"
Wife: "17."
Me: (*Read the 'things not to say' list.*)
Vet: "We are going to have to do some tests."
Wife: (*A look of terror.*)
Me: (*Read the list again.*)
Me: (*DON'T TELL YOUR WIFE YOU HAVE A LIST.*)

As Marli was taken away for her tests, I knew there was no point in me being there if I couldn't do what I wanted to do when I wasn't there the first time she went to the vet. The first time she went, I wanted to be there for my wife. To support her in her distress, to provide a shoulder and tissues for the inevitable tears and to provide the perfect quip at the perfect moment to at least make her smile for a second or two and remember how wonderful I was.

I stepped up. My shoulder was sturdy, my tissues were neatly packaged and primed and I commented (and made sure I got a closer look) on the woman that was on the TV in the reception area. (She was wearing a very low-cut dress.) Three out of three!

We waited for what seemed like hours. It wasn't, but by now it was past midnight, then the vet's examination room door opened.

Vet: "Marli?"
Wife: "Yes."

We walked in.
There was silence and it was deafening. Marli was on the examination table with a patch of fur missing.

Vet: "That is where we shaved her for her ultrasound. The tests show that she has—"

For some reason, there seemed to be a pause before her next words. There probably wasn't, after all this wasn't a game show, but to me, it seemed like just for that second, things slowed down.

Vet: "Cystitis."

Wife: (Hugh sigh of relief and a broad smile.)

Me: "Is it curable?"

Vet: "Yes. She is 17 but apart from the cystitis, she seems to be in good health."

Wife: (Still smiling, but now smiling and speaking to Marli in that annoying tone of voice.)

Me: (Happy to see my wife smiling, while trying to ignore the voice and the inevitable implications of the vet's bill.)

Marli: (A little bit of purring).

Vet: "She will need to be on a course of treatment, and we will need to see her again in a week."

Wife: (More annoying cat talk to Marli.)

Me: (The right and wrong emotions all at the same time.)

As we went to the counter to pay the bill, I was relieved that Marli would be OK and more importantly, I was relieved that my wife was happy again. More importantly than all that (and probably selfishly) I was relieved that I would not have to be supporting my wife as she dealt with what we both at one point thought was going to be a very very bad and sad evening.

Marli was going to be fine; my wife was going to be fine, and I was where I've always been, not quite understanding (or should that be appreciating) the pet thing but massively relieved. With my performance background, I was used to doing dress rehearsals, where you do things just as you would for the real event to ensure you are fully prepared for the opening night.

If this was a dress rehearsal, it was the first one, in 25 plus years of performing, I'd ever done where after it, I knew I would never be ready for the opening night or the curtain call.

Portugal.
Not a Bad Place to Wait!

The Covid 19 pandemic meant that I was able to continue working remotely so, while we had made the brave decision to move to another country and start a new life, in reality, we (or at least I) hadn't really escaped the shackles of a life working in Blighty.

Instead of working from a desk in England, having battled the cloudy or rain-soaked rush hour commuter hell that I had begun to despise, I was working from a desk in Portugal while looking out at blue skies and an inviting sun kissed pool.

Yes, it was an improvement, but I increasingly knew I was going to have to, at some point, cut the apron strings of the secure job that ultimately meant I couldn't actually go in the pool until 5.30pm (OK, some days it was 4.57ish!).

My wife's job was going well and, because she was so good at doing what she did, she was becoming increasingly busy getting extra work while I was getting equally stressed with a job I wasn't enjoying and the thought that eventually, I was going to be expected to return to Covid riddled Blighty.

As far as the house build was going, we were trying to push as hard as we could to get things moving forward but there were only so many times you could phone people and ask, with an increasingly optimistic and frustrated tone:

"Any news? Is there anything that we can be doing to move things forward?"

"Oh, you need another piece of paper, document or form that you didn't tell us you needed when we first asked you what we needed to give you!"

Along with that, there were some other frustrations:

"Ah, so when we asked you several times whether there would be a problem with having a borehole, and you said there would be no problems with having one (fortunate, because our whole plan for getting water rests on having a borehole) and that the council have said we can have a borehole, what you actually meant (or perhaps could have told us) was, firstly, as part of your role as architect, it is usually not you who deals with things like boreholes, the client does.
"Secondly (and perhaps more importantly) the council do not make the decision on whether we can have a bore hole, we have to make an application to another agency to ask them if we are allowed a borehole and, if they decide we can't have one, then we have to come up with another solution for getting water to our plot. So as we speak, we are not guaranteed to be allowed a borehole. Argh!"

During our visits to the vet, it was suggested that Marli might be suffering from stress. A diagnosis that was totally understandable, bearing in mind that all she did all day was sit, or lie, in a variety of comfy places, only moving to get a drink or snack from the variety of strategically placed water and food bowls that always seemed to appear from nowhere to ensure I kicked them over.

Despite this potentially stress inducing existence, Marli continued to make progress, with a few blips along the way. For blips read 500 euros of vet bills, tablets, solutions and treatments she had to take, hated taking and somehow knew when they had to be taken.

Her newfound ability to tell time resulted in twice daily chases around our rented apartment, her finding hidden or impossible to reach spaces in the room that was so full of our belongings that we could barely get in and therefore, we couldn't get her out so she could take her medicines.

Coupled to this were more of my wife's annoying tone of voice when she, or we, were finally able to grab hold of our newly intuitive feline. Upon capture, my wife would then proceed to cradle her, like a baby (cue annoying voice and cajoling) and begin the battle of wills that was trying to make sure the medicines we had paid so much for, rather than going all over our T-shirts, settee, or increasingly stained rug, actually went in Marli's mouth.

For an arthritic cat, nearly 18 years old (or 88 in human years), when the mood took her, there was still an Olympian like turn of speed, strength and agility that suggested (even if I did feel like I had better things to do than chase a cat around the house), the twice daily battle and trials and tribulations of getting her to take her medicines were proving worth it.

It was still the summer months, so while we waited for things to fall into place, working from home meant that as soon as it was clocking off time, we could either take the 30minute drive to one of four beaches we had access to, or just jump in the pool. We did a lot of both. We liked going to the beach.

It was novel, relaxing and exactly one of the things we were looking forward to when we moved. There was something about hearing the waves that made even the most stressful day disappear and, if the waves, coupled with a cold beer and a smiling happy wife didn't do it, bikini clad sun seekers, in all shapes and sizes, went some way to providing that little bit of an extra stress buster.

Perhaps it was because the Portuguese were used to it, so for them it was not a thing, but for me, seeing people feeling free and comfortable enough to not worry about what others think, in terms of body image, was and is liberating and so, the beach trips, for a variety of reasons, had many positives.

While waiting for news, we also decided we should take advantage of our location. Sao Bras de Alportel, where we had decided to set up home, is approximately 42mins from the Spanish border and, with tales of how everything is much cheaper in Spain, we decided to go and see for ourselves.

The drive was quick, the drive took in the bridge that had caused me so much stress and sweat the first time we crossed it and the drive included apparently funny jibes from my wife as to my well-being.

Nevertheless, we crossed the border, and we were in Spain. One of the best things about going was being able to tell our folks back home that we were going to Spain for the day, something we still get a kick out of being able to say and do and another reason why we moved. We had a great day, did lots of shopping and yes, things were a lot cheaper. This prompted the question:

Me: "Why didn't we move here, instead of Portugal?"
Wife: "Because we like Portugal."

Once again, my wife was right (I hate having to say that!) but we will definitely be going to Spain more often.

During the summer months, we had our first visitor from England. Dave, my friend who had for many years holidayed in Portugal and so took a keen interest in our adventure, arrived along with his daughter, for their annual two-week break.

We were still bound by Covid restrictions so, with social distancing in full force, we met for beers, food, a few more beers and plenty of laughs. The first one being Dave arriving with a cool box full of 'sem alcool' beers. His face, when I told him it meant 'non-alcoholic' was a picture that became even more funny when he realised, I wasn't joking.

Luckily, my time in Portugal had meant I had picked up a bit of the lingo, so my cool box was well stocked with 'com alcool' beers and so we dived straight in.

Dave is an electrician and so not only was he interested in our Portuguese adventure, but he also knew lots about the construction industry, house building and all things building related. He was keen to see our plans and the land he had heard so much about and so, in between beers, food and more beers, and while my wife stayed behind to sort out the food (her choice, not mine) me, Dave and his daughter went to see exactly what I'd been talking about for the last year or more.

Neither I nor my wife are the type of people to really care about what others think. We've always done what we've wanted to do, or thought was best, regardless of whether others thought it was a good idea or not.

That said, for some reason I, and I think my wife, maybe because he knew about building and things, and a few years earlier had toyed, hoped and seriously investigated the idea of doing something similar in Portugal, only to be thwarted by finances, really wanted Dave to not only like the land and our plans, but to also share our vision and give his seal of approval to the whole shebang.

After all, seeing as he (so far) was the only person who had been given an open invitation to visit us, we wanted him to see where he would be coming to for the future rugby watching weekends and beer drinking breaks I was looking forward to once the house was finished.

As we drove to the land, I was slightly nervous about what he would think and say. Would he like it? Would he think we had wasted our money on a dud project? Would he think I had been talking large about something that just wasn't that great that he would immediately see problems with and be glad it wasn't him?

As we arrived, and each stepped out of our respective cars, the first thing I heard was his daughter say, "what a great drive up here." So far so good and, I'm not sure what this said about me but, as I proceeded to show them round the land and discussed our plans, showed them where the goats were going to be housed and where Rocky and Adrian would live, the look of surprise about just how good the land was (and the look of envy in their eye) gave me a warm feeling of knowing we were doing something good, something many people could only dream of doing.

To give them credit, it wasn't long before firstly his daughter said, "Wow, this is amazing," and while looking at her dad, said, "He's so jealous," before Dave himself gave the approval I always knew I didn't need, but always knew I very much wanted.

Dave: "I'm soooo jealous!"
Me: "When you come to stay, this is where your room will be."

As we looked around the land, Dave and his daughter took in the views and Dave gave me the benefit of his experience as we discussed options for retaining walls, lighting, fencing, drainage and lots of other glamorous topics. As we talked, I felt warmer and warmer and even more excited at the prospect of what we were doing and, after a bit more building talk and expressions of envy, so Dave could show his wife what she would be missing out on and where he would be coming to for our future weekend jaunts, it was time for a few photos.

Then they had a final wistful look at the views before we headed back to continue with more beers, some food, some laughs and a few more beers. Dave and his daughter returned back to the UK and sent the obligatory text, with the UK's gloomy weather forecast for the following week and tales of woolly socks and central heating.

We (and especially me) buoyed by my mate's approval (or should that be envy?) resumed our push for progress with the build. This meant that we had to start looking for builders and getting quotes so that, when we did eventually hear something, we were ready to go to the next step.

So, the process of sourcing builders began with the usual Facebook trawl for recommendations, customer nightmare stories, taking numbers from the side of vans (and in some cases photos, accompanied by understandable funny looks from passers-by) and, infuriatingly, trying to avoid 'ET', not the bicycle riding alien, but the 'Expat Tax'.

The 'Expat Tax' is where builders make assumptions about customers and as a result, submit inflated building quotes simply on the basis that:

A. You want to build in the Algarve.
B. Therefore, you must be rich.
C. You can afford it.

Well in our case, their algebra was well off (perhaps that's why they are builders?) and we both enjoyed the look on the faces of the 'ET' type builders we talked to when, as we dismissed them and waved goodbye, they realised firstly, we only fulfilled the A part of three ET criteria and secondly (and perhaps more importantly) A minus B did not equal C.

It was during this tendering for the job phase that the reality of another peculiarity within the Portuguese planning system struck a costly blow. Me and my wife like showers and never take baths so we had not intended to have any bathrooms with a bath in them.

Enter Portuguese planning law. *All new constructions must have at least one full bathroom suite, including a bath and a bidet.* This meant we had to stand the costs of buying and fitting a bath and bidet that we never wanted and knew would never get used.

Bearing in mind one of the quotes we received estimated the cost of supplying and fitting a bath at 500 euros, we were not pleased with this requirement. This was coupled with the compulsory tiling of every bathroom to a height of at least 1.5m, every bathroom needing to be wheelchair accessible, regardless of whether it was on the ground, first or higher floor and regardless of whether there were ramps to access those floors.

There was also a requirement for compulsory TV sockets in bedrooms (even though we hate the idea of a TV in the bedroom). Despite many conversations with our new architect, we had no option but to comply and deal with having to pay for things we did not want.

We decided to get three quotes in total. There is nothing like seeing things in black and white with figures on a page, so when the quotes came, there was an overwhelming feeling that things were getting serious. Alongside that, the feeling that I would want to be in and around every aspect of the build process began to grow and grow.

How could I keep working, even if it was remotely, with this life changing thing happening and me not being there to help (even though some may suggest, hinder) the process. Would I be able to stay chained to a computer or be required to attend online meetings I didn't care about, while decisions were being made about where to put the bath, bidet, or the TV sockets we didn't want.

There was much soul searching, not to mention calculations on whether we could afford to do things if I stopped working. Would my new drill, slung from my tool belt, save the day, and the required euros, to enable me to say that's it, I'm leaving work.

If I continued to work in Blighty, then I wouldn't have the time to perhaps generate opportunities here in Portugal and I would be forever in the limbo of, either virtually or in reality wanting to be here but having to be there.

As we analysed the quotes and asked ourselves many questions, including:

"Why are things always so much more expensive than you want them to be?"
"Why is it so expensive to dig holes?"
"Why is it that the one you want is usually the most expensive?"
"Why do the Portuguese insist on 23% VAT, or IVA, as they call it?"
"Why do we have to pay for a bloomin' bidet?"

Finally, we made a decision. I was going to resign, so I did. Just like that. Wrote the email, clicked send and immediately felt better. We were doing this, and we were going to do it properly. I was now officially living in Portugal full-time and, as luck would have it, on the day I sent the resignation email. I started to get some offers of work right here.

Whether or not we made the right decision, only time would tell but as we picked up speed into the build, resigning seemed to have been the right choice. We also made a decision about a builder and, after analysing our three quotes, with one seemingly coming straight out of a Spielberg movie, in that it was 120,000 euros higher than the other two!

We went with a builder that was recommended by the architect. So we were moving forward, albeit very slowly and begrudgingly accepting the fact that if we were going to do things properly, then we had to take on board the Portuguese rules of building and we were going to have to come to terms with buying a bidet. So, imagine our surprise when one morning we awoke to find a discarded bathroom item next to the pool.

Wife: "Is that a bidet?"
Me: "I think it is."
Wife to Landlady: "Is that a bidet?"
Landlady: "Yes, we're getting rid of it."
Me: "Can we have it? We have to put one in our house even though—yadda yadda yadda!"
Landlady: "Yes, course you can, it's got a crack in it though."
Wife: "Doesn't matter, we're going to take it out once the house has been inspected."
Landlady: "I've got the taps as well if you want them."
Both of us: "YES, PLEASE."

So at last, it felt like things were moving forward. It had been a year since we began our journey from Huddersfield, only to return for my wallet, have a row and then leave again, but now to add to our dreams, hopes, frustrations, naivety and remarkably patient architect, we had my mate's approval, a possibly stressed but recuperating cat, 500 euros less to spend on the house, no depressing job back in Blighty, a builder and a bidet.

We Can Build in Portugal

Our builder was based locally and was well-known as having a good reputation. He had shown us some of his previous work and also invited us to his office. We felt confident that he was the right one for us and in the event he wasn't, we would know exactly where to go to kick up a fuss.

Choosing your builder is always a big step but perhaps more so under the Portuguese system for building. Without a named builder, to put on your construction licence application, you can't get a construction licence and without a construction licence, you can't start building.

With that in mind, you don't want to be in the position to have to change builder mid-project because that would mean going through the construction licence application process again (causing inevitable delays), so getting the right builder and therefore, the right name on the licence first time was very important.

You will have to keep reading to see whether we had the right name on the licence but for now, and due to Covid restrictions and the mandatory wearing of masks, we were confident enough to hand over a considerable amount of money to a guy whose face we had never actually seen.

Having the builder in place also meant we could add him to our list of 'people to get excited about when their name comes up on your phone, text or email'. The process of trying to get a house built was a lengthy one and every conversation, email or correspondence with any protagonist, or even minor player in the process, felt like you were one step closer.

Having this name to add to the cast list meant that sure enough, we were getting very close to the opening of act 1, scene 1, of our very own feature length epic. At times, our architect was probably on the verge of adding the phrase 'extremely patient' to his CV and list of skills, as we, in his words, "Change your minds very often."

Although for us, it was more of a case of just considering the options. Anyway, I think the architect was pleased to have the builder on board as a partner to work with and, probably more importantly, as another option for us when he forgot he had the skill of being extremely patient.

We now had everything in place. All we needed was the construction licence and we would be good to go. Each time the builder's or architect's name, came up on our phones email, etc. we each got excited, only for it to be another document to sign, another amendment, or something trivial. Then we got a call from the architect.

Architect: "The construction licence is ready, so you just have to pick it up at the council office."

The moment we had been waiting for, the moment we had been focused on for months and when the call came, I'm not sure what we were expecting, but there was no fanfare, dancing girls or pom-poms, there was however, a hefty cost for the licence.

We knew we would have to pay for it, but we weren't quite prepared for the actual amount. In the end, the celebrations for getting the licence were definitely muted as a result of the unexpected but necessary re-calibration of our finances. We did chuckle though when we realised some of the benefits of being in a small town where everybody knew each other.

Our architect told me that when I went to get the licence, I had parked in the mayor's parking place and if I did it again, I would get a fine, but seeing as he knew the mayor and the mayor knew we were excited about getting our licence, he had let it go and had parked somewhere else. I hoped the walk did him good.

So we had our licence, we had our builder and we agreed on a start date for the build. We also had, of course, one last document to sign, which informed the council of when the actual momentous day was.

We had gone from first drawings to getting a construction licence in approximately 8 months, which, in light of the horror stories we had heard, and those choruses of 'Things Take Time, This is Portugal', was by any standards pretty fast and probably faster than if we had been building something in England. For that we will be forever grateful to our architect.

Before the start date, we decided to go for a drive to a posh part of town where all of the houses were very plush, worth lots of money, and quite frankly were a bit ugly, but we thought we might get some ideas for our own impending Algarve dream house. As we were driving around and discussing the fact that money doesn't equal taste, we were flagged down by an elderly gentleman who had noticed our GB plates and so knew we were from England.

We passed the time of day and talked a little bit about each other and how we had both managed to end up in Portugal. He had the kind of accent that immediately made you think public school, establishment, or Hugh Grant in most of his films. Basically, he was really posh. So posh that when referring to his parents, he called them 'Mummy and Daddy'.

It turned out that he was a member of the House of the Lords, had been living in Portugal for 30 years and was in the process of starting a new business venture. We exchanged numbers, as you do, and thought no more of it, except the fact that as soon as we got home, we Googled him.

Sure enough, he was who he said he was and was indeed Lord Somebody the 3rd Viscount of somewhere and his Google profile was accompanied by pictures of him with various government ministers from a variety of countries in which he had been instrumental in affecting change and conducting serious business deals.

As the days passed, we exchanged various text and WhatsApp messages and, before you know it, he was asking me to consult on his parliamentary questions, write the text for them and, as he asked the questions I had written, giving me the chance to watch him in action in the House of Lords.

I'm not sure who 'they' were but, 'they' do say that opportunity strikes in the unlikeliest of places and it appeared that 'they' were right. When we set out for our drive that morning, I never imagined it would end up with meeting a Lord and I certainly never imagined I would be writing questions that would be heard and considered by government ministers and members of parliament.

It then transpired he was looking for someone to join him in his business venture and wondered whether I would consider it. I'd just given up a job so I could concentrate on our impending build (and I was definitely getting used to not working) and there I was being offered a job right here in Portugal. I knew I didn't want to be working full-time, but I also knew this was an opportunity that had somehow fallen in my lap and so couldn't be passed up and so I accepted his invitation. I now had a job (albeit part-time so I could devote some time to the build).

The start date for the build arrived and to say we were excited was perhaps a slight under-statement. Despite the slight chill (that in my mind just made it even more romantic), it was a gloriously sunny day. We had been planning, discussing, designing, worrying, re-discussing, re-planning, re-designing and continually worrying about this day for a long time and now it was finally here.

We arrived on site just in time to have our camera ready to see the JCB make the first incision into our plot of land. Finally, we had started.

Me and Wife: Smile, kiss, cuddle, kiss, smile, cuddle.

Me: Immature but serious comments about christening rooms and balconies.

Wife: Laugh, smile, coy giggle, glint in her eye.

Me and Wife: Smile, kiss, cuddle, kiss, smile, cuddle.

Wife: Classy slurp of champagne straight from the bottle.

Me and Wife: Champagne toast to each other (this time with glasses).

Wife: Another classy slurp straight from the bottle.

Yes, we had been planning this for at least two years, but in actual fact we had wanted to build our own house for more than that and this was the culmination of something like 12 years of dreaming and planning. All those trips to DIY stores, building magazines, fancy designs, trade shows, TV programmes of excited self-builders and now it was us, on site, in wheelies, with camera in hand, watching the first stages of our own dream build taking place. Other than getting married and then moving to Portugal, this was the best thing we had ever done.

By the end of the first day, we were both surprised by just how much the JCB had done and we could see exactly where our house was going to be. We also thought that now building had started, there would be builders on site every day and that I would be there with my blue hard hat that (in preparation for this very moment) my wife had bought me for a birthday present.

In reality, for the next week it rained and rained heavily and so there was nothing going on onsite. So we had started in a blaze of glory and then come to an abrupt hiatus. There was nothing happening, no sign of builders and no sign of the materials that our large sum of up-front money was supposed to be buying.

There was, on my part at least, a few jitters about whether we had indeed chosen a reputable builder, whether we had paid a large sum of money just for a digger to come for one day and then never be seen again and whether I was going to have to make use of my knowledge of the location of the builder's office.

Our fears were short lived and sure enough, as the weather improved, so did the frequency of seeing builders on site. It quickly became apparent that firstly, we had chosen a good builder and secondly, for the time being at least, the builders had no need for my over enthusiasm, hard hat, tool belt and questionable skills.

It also became apparent that the culture of building sites in Portugal was very different to that in England. In England, you see those signs about Health and Safety and the need to have the correct safety equipment and boots, etc. otherwise you would not be able to work.

Portugal was a little different. It seemed to be on site in Portugal all you needed were some of the right skills, a good pair of sunglasses and for your lunch break, a couple of beers in your bag.

At this point, I don't want to give the impression that the builder and his team were not expertly skilled and professional, because they were and are, but their relaxed approach to work was a breath of fresh air and, before I turned up in my Builders.com outfit (complete with shiny new hard hat, protective goggles, boots and tool belt), I'm glad I realised the Portuguese way of doing things.

We were in good hands and those hands didn't need gloves, or the restraint of rules. They just needed the freedom to do what they do, in the way they do it, assisted by a couple of beers at lunch time. Perfect.

Throughout this exciting time for us, Marli had kept to her usual cool, calm and collected self (with the occasional dart across the carpet). What had been most pleasing was that there had been no trips to the vets although what had been less pleasing was her inability to learn that, like it or not, medicine that wasn't cheap had to be taken and so medicine would be taken.

We naively thought that she might get used to it, or that we might get better at administering it. Neither came to fruition and so the daily Greek-Roman wrestling match of medicine time continued. So far, I think the scores are even but that might be wishful thinking on our part.

One slightly worryingly thing was that she developed quite a pronounced limp to one of her back legs that, when she walked, made her look like either John Wayne (in his cowboy heyday), Keyser Soze (in the movie The Usual Suspects) or a black guy with the rhythm and soul of the Caribbean in his back pocket.

When we first found her, all those years ago, she had a broken pelvis and it seems that 18 years later, this was coming back to haunt her. Nevertheless, although her dancing days may have been few and far between, she certainly mastered the art of, as soon as I got up, jumping into my place on the sofa and then looking very put out when she was asked to move or, (as was inevitably the case), moved.

My wife still spoke to her in that annoying voice and we think Marli (and my wife when it suited her) may have gone a little bit deaf, although there were only signs of that when I talked to them. Marli also developed quite a loud voice, which was usually put to use in the middle of the night.

Lastly, while sleeping in my place on the sofa, she had also mastered the art of curling up in a ball, which had the effect of melting my wife's heart and making me look like the bad guy when I even suggested that she might have to move so that I could sit down.

Despite the leg, Marli's move to Portugal, just like ours, seemed to be going just fine.

We Really Are Building in Portugal

Once we actually started building, I thought we would give up on all those TV programmes we had been watching for what seemed like forever. As we dreamed of actually doing it ourselves, we used to watch any programme with the words 'House', 'Build', 'Garden' (or any combination of them) in the title.

Now, we were doing it ourselves; weirdly, our appetite for these programmes seemed as avid as ever (well, mine at least). I still couldn't get enough of them, as I relived stories of self builds, and the trials and tribulations of couples just like us, with their champagne ideas and lemonade budgets (or more money than we could ever dream of), as they joined the Self-Builder's club and rode the SB roller coaster. Well now, we had our own membership cards and we were definitely cashing in our ticket to ride.

Watching, and re-watching these programmes brought back many memories of us saying 'if only', but as well as that, as we judged our own progress against all the couples we had seen, these programmes inspired us to make sure we were making the most of every opportunity and idea and, more importantly, enjoying every moment.

Being able to compare our experiences with the experiences of 'the people on the telly' was fun and allowed us to keep our own emotions in check. We realised that although we were only a few months into our build; we were progressing nicely, had not had to double our groundworks budget (like so many of the projects we had seen), we had a good team of builders and, as we realised the dream that we shared with all of those couples in all of those programmes, we were in a good place.

We were very lucky (although we often made our own luck) and we were building our dream. The one downside however, was that in all these programmes, you got to see the finished product within the hour. Our finished product was going to take just a little bit longer than that.

With my flask of coffee and a spring in my step, on most days I went to the building site. I wanted to be able to see the process day by day and I wanted to see our house constructed stage by stage. It was fascinating, although I'm not sure what the builders thought about the chap who obviously had so much time on his hands, he could afford to stand around a building site for the best part of a day, drinking coffee.

I had come to terms with not seeing my plan of 'helping the builders' come to fruition and so I was content just to watch and see the guys in action and I must admit, despite feeling a little useless, I was enjoying watching other people work.

Being on site, on an almost daily basis, allowed me to see where we had either under, or over thought something, or where, as opposed to an architect's drawing, now that we could actually see it in real life, we wanted to change our minds or make better use of the land or develop our original idea.

For us, the building process was always going to be just that, a process, during which ideas could be developed and changes could be made. Unfortunately, our architect seemed to think that the building process should be, and therefore was going to be, the completion of the original (or his original) idea, without any changes. So we had reached the first bump in the road with many conversations following this pattern.

> **Us:** "Hi Architect, we have been thinking."
> **Architect:** Huge sigh, huffing and puffing.
> **Us:** "We would like to change this, that, the other."
> **Architect**: "Why do you want to change this? I don't agree."
> **Us** (to ourselves): "Do you think he doesn't agree because he doesn't want to have to do more drawings?"
> **Architect**: "If it were my house, I wouldn't do that."
> **Us:** "Does that mean it is a bad idea? Here is our rationale for wanting to change things."
> **Architect:** (often grudgingly, as he realised we were not asking for things on a whim) "OK, I can see what you mean with this, but we have to be careful because everything must be agreed by the council. This will mean the build will cost more money."

Unlike the UK (as it had been explained to us), Portuguese homeowners were not allowed 'Permitted Development Rights'. All building changes, and this was especially true of new builds that needed a habitation licence for them to be fully legal, must get council approval and must match the project that was initially given permission for. Therefore, making changes could land you in hot water when the council did their final inspection.

The usual end, or last word, on these conversations usually fell into one of the following:

Us (to ourselves): "Do you think he is a little bit arrogant and is not used to people questioning him and so he is using the council as an excuse?"

Or

"Actually, he makes a good point there, shall we leave it as it is?"

Or

"No. We would like this to be changed, please."

Either way, the first few months of the build had shown us many things; we were going to want the scope to make changes, our architect didn't want to afford us the scope to make changes and therefore, there was the potential for our British 'the customer is always right' culture to be at odds with the Portuguese way of doing things.

There was also the potential for our previously amicable relations to sour. It was also becoming clear that if relations were not to sour, we had to decide that our architect wasn't rude but instead, there was a language and culture gap that we had to be aware of.

Regardless of this, what was very clear was that everyone who had so far seen the build, it's positioning on the land, and its potential, had, without exception, said what a great house it looked. We agreed with them and for that we had to be grateful to our architect and the team of builders.

For the early stages of the build, working under the guidance of the main builder, we had subcontractors. They were responsible for the initial wood shuttering and iron work that would support the concrete. Although occasionally, there were a few new faces, generally, we had the same team of guys.

That team consisted of a the fat bald one with a cute little hat, whose belly hung over his tool belt, one who always seemed to be in a bad mood, one who was friendly and always said, "Bom Dia," when I arrived on site, a black guy who never said anything, but always wore clean white trainers to work before changing into wellies or work boots, and the guy who did the labouring type jobs such as moving piles of stones from point A to Point B with only a shovel or bucket to do it with.

To look at them, they were never going to appear in 'Builders Weekly', but I was quickly beginning to realise they had the necessary minerals to build a good-looking house and, at this point at least, our dream was in their hands.

I wanted to try and make sure that I could go to the site and feel, not only welcome, but also that the builders didn't resent me being there. I'm not sure why this was important to me, but it was. Every morning when I arrived on site, the fact that I still didn't quite believe we were actually doing it, ensured that I had a smile on my face and a sense of enthusiasm for every single piece of action, wood, hammer blow and especially for the JCB.

I loved the JCB and its ability to get in and out of seemingly impossible places and its ability to, in one day, make me re-evaluate the land and how things were going to eventually look. When we'd watched all those housey programmes I especially liked the ones where there was a whole team of people doing the hard graft. They always seemed to have a clear and sizeable budget, the correct power tools and most importantly of all, a mini digger that was often operated by the people or person whose house or project was being built. I was very much looking forward it being my turn to drive a mini digger.

So far, the closet I'd come to living the mini digger dream was when I went to try and hire one. For some reason, I thought I could go to a Portuguese mini digger hire place, give them the dates I wanted it, they would deliver it, then leave me to play at being a proper builder, (getting some good video footage to boot). Then the mini digger hire guy would collect, what had become my friend, there would be a tearful goodbye, but both the mini digger and his rightful owner would feel the pride of serving the international community of The Algarve. To top it all off, we'd be doing our bit to support a local business. (I don't think I've left anything out).

The day we went to hire a mini digger went something like this:

Me: "Bom DiA" (Good morning—You can get the boy out of Yorkshire, but his accent will always have a hard A)

Mini Digger Guy (MDG): Did not even acknowledge I'd come into the shop.

ME: Bom DiA, Gost de (*"I would like"-,* although that was completely wrong, but I knew it was 'Gosto' or was it

'Gosta' for like?) **Vossa** ("Your"—again, probably not quite correct but I was going with it because when we'd been watching some of the Anglo/American TV channels and programmes that were now available to us, whenever there was the word "Vossa" in the subtitles it seemed to coincide with one of the characters saying 'your'). **Large pointing motion in the direction of the mini diggers on display in the yard.** At this point, rather than going with my obvious command of the Portuguese language, I went with common sense. My strategy was to play safe. He was a mini digger hire guy and I had come to his mini digger hire shop to hire a mini digger; therefore, the decision was taken that what was needed was a strong pointy gesture.

MDG: Bom Dia (said properly, but somehow not how it sounded on the Portuguese language CDs we bought)
Me: Roughly the same as last time but feeling a little more confident.
MDG: (a little bit more interest now)
Me: Falar English? (no explanation needed)
MDG: A little.
Me: (Big sigh of relief. Things were going well)

We went outside to where the diggers were and it seemed my fluency in Eng-guese was working, because the mini digger guy seemed convinced that I knew what I was doing when it came to mini diggers. As we walked around each machine, he described its capabilities, asked me questions about tonnage, and asked my opinion of the different models. Unfortunately, what happened next did not move negotiations closer to securing that much-coveted video footage.

I won't take up your time reading my ridiculously bad attempts to appear in the least bit knowledgeable about the Portuguese language and mini diggers. I felt the main thing was that I was trying. The next step of what I was now calling 'Operation Video Footage', was to stay calm, try not to come across as *Del Boy on OL-Li-Day* (a character from a very popular British TV sitcom) and we'd have our landscaping done in no time.

Me:

- Asking a stupid question, that someone who knew what they were doing would know the answer to.
- Jumping into a digger then starting to sing "Bob the Builder"
- "How fast does it go?"

It was pretty obvious I had no clue.

MDG: No
Me: I'll be careful!
MDG: No
Me: (about to say something that I felt sure would convince him)

MDG: No.

Then the guy proceeded to tell me, in really good English, why I couldn't hire a mini digger and why I would probably injure myself or worst.

Me: (Thinking) So you can speak English then?

I was not going to get my video footage; this was not going to be as easy as first thought and this was clearly a bad idea in the first place. I trundled back to the car.

Wife: How did you get on?

Me: He won't let me have one.

Wife: All well, not to worry.

Me: (Thinking about all the digging that lay ahead and seeing my dream fade away) Would have been nice though!

Wife: Nevermind.

(For some reason Alan Bennet comes to mind. Furthermore, I could tell she was relieved)

On reflection, I would question the sanity of anyone who would give me the keys to a JCB (mini or otherwise) and, despite me looking for evidence of madness, our JCB driver seemed to be of sound mind. It was very clear, very quickly, and I had to come to terms with the fact, there was never going to be a 'my turn' moment.

Nonetheless, every morning when I arrived, the fat bald one barely said hello, the grumpy one remained grumpy, the black guy still never spoke, and the friendly one who, as I found out, spoke French was still friendly.

The fact he spoke French meant that firstly (as I tried frantically to remember my high school French lessons), Mr Bentley (my French teacher) was right. The day he had prophesied had finally arrived and given my time again, I would indeed avert my gaze from the variety of pretty females in my French classes and give my full concentration to his verb conjugations.

I desperately wanted to show that I was not one of those English folks who (while hoping whoever they were talking to could speak some English), never bothered to learn the language of the country they have moved to. I threw myself into conversation in what could only be described as Fren-tugese-lish, during which I marvelled at his bilingual ability and I muddled through, dropping in the odd English word in the hope that he was in fact tri-lingual.

My Portuguese was getting better but it was still woefully bad and luckily, the friendly one took pity on me. The labouring guy was also quite friendly and one day, as I helped him with his stone moving duties, he revealed he was originally from Pakistan and had a master's degree in economics and was hoping to, in the next few years, move to Scandinavia to pursue his economic ambitions.

If I didn't already know it, here was living proof that you just never knew who you were dealing with so best not to make too many judgements about people. That being said, my judgement on the other three remained the same.

In an attempt to further ingratiate myself with my team of crack builders and tradesmen, I initiated 'Cerveja, Sexta-Fiera' or, for those who, unlike myself, do not speak Portuguese, 'Beer Friday'. This meant every Friday I would go to the site and hand out cans of beer just to say thanks for their work that week and in general.

So every Friday, the fat bald one still had his cute hat and belly hanging over his tool belt, now looked forward to my contribution to his waistline, the grumpy one now said, "Ah beer, give to me, please," and now smiled (to reveal he had few teeth).

The black guy said, "Obrigado," (Thank you) and nothing else. I think the labouring guy was still trying to figure me out, but with a masters in economics, I was surprised it was taking him so long. The friendly one was just that bit friendlier as he tried to persuade me there should be a 'Cerveja Segunda, Terca, Quinta, and Quarta'.

Nevertheless, we were very appreciative for their work and even though they didn't like rain (so on rainy days, nothing got done) they were cracking on and we were seeing our dream being realised.

During the whole process of buying the land, designing the house, etc. we always knew that we wanted a borehole. Even though our architect said it wouldn't be a problem (although he does not decide such things) and our planning permission confirmed our project included one and said we could have one, we still hadn't had consent from the government agency that authorised the installation of one.

This meant that despite all our planning, we could still be told we weren't allowed one and we would have to go back to square one with regards to a water supply. The rural location in which we were building had a variety of water stations that provided drinking water and while we were growing things, we would make the short walk, or drive to fill our water container.

As romantic as that notion seemed, our dream of building a house did not include having to go and fetch water on a daily basis, so not having authorisation for the borehole was an issue that was still outstanding and had not been resolved.

Alongside needing permission, this was Portugal, so it wasn't that simple. Firstly, we had to apply to make an application. This cost money. Then we had to make an application. This cost money. Then we had to wait for someone to survey the land and determine whether there was an existing borehole within a 100m radius of the one we were planning.

If one was found, we would need the consent of the land and borehole owner before we could get permission for our own. On top of that, although we had a rough estimation of the cost, we didn't really know what it would cost and so its price had the potential to have an impact on everything else. Our discussions on this topic went roughly like this:

Me: "I hope we can get this borehole."

Wife: "Me too, but I think it won't be cheap."

Me: "What if the price is astronomical?"

Wife: "What choice do we have? We can buy water, but we don't want that."

Me: "We'll just have to make savings in other areas, although at the moment we are over budget and we still have no bathrooms, kitchen, flooring, pool tiles or fencing."

Wife: "Hmmm!"

Me: (*Coming from a place of possibly flawed masculinity and feeling like it was always my responsibility to provide the financial solutions for my family, but not having any credible answer at that present moment.*) "Don't worry darling, we'll sort it."

To add to this, on a walk near our soon to be dream house, we met our near neighbours. On the face of it, they seemed nice. A Dutch couple, both retired and both a bit interested/nosey about what we were doing.

Newly met Neighbours: "Ah, you're having a borehole? We thought of having one but decided they were too expensive. They're very expensive, you know?"

I've since decided that they were OK and just being friendly and I was perhaps being my usual meeting new people grumpy person.

We were put in touch with a borehole company and, after speaking to the company's owner (who was a really nice guy), they sent us an estimate for the work. It was of course minus the additions we would need, for example a pump, and it came with the caveat that the estimate was per metre of digging and assumed we could use the cheapest components. So we budgeted for that amount and hoped for the best.

We eventually got permission to have a borehole and the company came and did the work. Guess what? They had to dig deeper than they imagined, we could not use the cheapest components, and so therefore had to use the most expensive ones and the total cost was nearly double what we had budgeted for.

To be honest, I'm still coming to terms with the price and will probably struggle for some time to come. The fact that we had a better-than-expected water pressure and would easily be able to pump more than 5000 litres a day, did not cut much ice in helping me cope. I was hoping the adage 'there is always tomorrow' would kick in, but all I seemed to get, and still get, was 'tomorrow never comes'.

As I'd been going to the building site, my wife and Marli had been staying at the place we are renting. During the first few months of building, Portugal, due to Covid, had remained in lockdown, and so my wife had been working from home. What had been really interesting was her view of what was happening.

When we weren't building, whenever I went to the site, she would say, "Are you going to the land?" In those first few months of building, she asked, "Are you going to the build today?" We both looked forward to, "Are you going to the house today?" And eventually, "We are going home today."

My wife working from home had many benefits. We got to have lazy mornings, breakfast together, lunch together and, during the day, we got to pretend we were not copping a feel as we 'accidentally' brushed past one another in our now *can't wait to be in our own house* small kitchenette.

For my wife, working from home consisted of teaching sessions using Zoom. Zoom was the application that before Covid, nobody had heard of and since Covid, had become an indispensable staple of everyday life.

During these sessions, a la those famous Joyce Grenfell monologues, I heard several children's names, usually followed by, "stop putting that in there", "are you listening to me?" "Stop hitting your little brother", or "Nicolas, Jack, Ahmed, Tom, Dick, Harry, or, Sophia, Amelia, Bethany, Mary Jane, stop playing with (insert random computer function) and pay attention."

To be honest, it was usually the boys that gave her hassle and I couldn't help but have a wry smile as I remembered my own school days and the troubles I used to cause Mrs Hegarty, Mrs North, Mrs Gregory and some of the other teachers I had. Funnily enough, I never ever messed with Mrs Tordoff! Nobody messed with Mrs Tordoff.

The place we were renting basically had two rooms, the bedroom and the kitchen diner. This meant, while I was in the kitchen diner, watching housey programmes or doing my work (usually the former), my wife was in the bedroom as she did her work.

This also meant that Marli felt the need to be with her and so, even though I didn't like her being in the bedroom, the sight of her curled up on the bed, or stretched out while giving me a look that I'm sure said, "Nah nah na nah nah. Look at me! I'm on the bed again," was a regular sight and something I was learning, however begrudgingly, to put up with.

The Zoom sessions also saw Marli develop a taste for taking a starring role on camera and so, as my wife taught, I frequently heard the refrain of, "ah, isn't she cute," as Marli, despite the inspiring lesson my wife was trying to deliver, took centre stage for her increasingly frequent camera close ups.

To be honest, Marli had the ability to look really cute and while she was staying well away from the vet, and therefore not giving us any vet bills and looking blissfully happy with her new 'on camera' persona, we were, all three of us, happy with the way things were going.

Raised Beds in Portugal

Me: "Is that blood on the floor?"
Wife: "Where?"
Me: "There. On the bathroom mat. Where's Marli?"
Wife: "Have you seen any blood anywhere else?"
Me: "No, but where's Marli?"

Cue Marli's entrance, as she appeared, without a care in the world, to take up her residency on the bed.

Wife: "Ah, there she is. She looks OK."

We worryingly started the search for more evidence of blood, or episodes of cat vomit, while we kept an eye on Marli. For her part, Marli just stared at us as if to say 'What's all the fuss about. Could you keep it down, I'm trying to sleep'.

The search revealed no more evidence of blood or vomit and, as we breathed a sigh of relief, my wife went to investigate the suspicious red marks on the bathroom mat.

Wife: "I don't think it's blood."
Me: "Why not?"

Wife: "It smells fruity."

The panic was over. It wasn't blood after all and, as my wife's keen nose was able to point out, I had trodden on a rogue strawberry that had been dropped on the floor during our morning breakfast juicing routine. This was the stain on the bathroom mat.

Two Weeks Earlier.

My wife's job had gone from strength to strength, so much so, that her role as music specialist had been expanded to that of Head of the Reception year group. This meant that she was now working five days a week and boy, did I know it. It seemed like every time she spoke, every sentence started with:

"Now I'm working full time, will you do this, that and the other."
"Now I'm working full time, I've left a list of things that need doing, so can you do them today please."
"Now I'm working full time, what am I having for dinner?"
"Now I'm working full time, I won't have a chance to do this, or that, or the other, so can you do it."

(You will notice the lack of question marks. Why, because when she said these things, they never sounded like questions).
"Now I'm working full time, you said that when I started working full time, you would help out more around the house."

My wife was right. I did say I would help out more around the house, and I WAS, it just somehow seemed to be not noticed. I'd even taken to doing the ironing and cleaning my own bathroom. Jobs that were previously, and most definitely, on the 'pink list'. Suffice to say, my wife's new responsibilities had meant a shift in our 'division of labour' and the balance was certainly tipping.

Her having to go to work every day had put a serious dent in our lazy morning routine and although we were always early risers, the need for her to actually get out of the house meant that mornings were now run to a strict timetable. 7am, up, showered, breakfast juicing, breakfast and then a kiss goodbye, in what seemed like the reverse of a scene from the 1960s, in which I stayed at home and she went out to work.

I didn't really stay at home all day, because I was either up on the site, or actually working myself but anyway, as I waved her off each morning, it did sometimes feel like all I needed was a pinny and I'd be set for my new 'stay at home' role.

It was on one such regimented morning, in between juicing and breakfast, that Marli strolled into the kitchen and it was obvious things were not right. Yes, there was her limp, but this time it was accompanied by a side to side swaying, some unseemly meows (actually squeaks, she's never been able to meow), and then heaving, after which, there was vomiting.

Marli has always been one of those cats that vomits. Apparently, according to my wife, some cats were like this and they often ate grass to make themselves vomit to get rid of hairballs. Marli had the quirky habit of never just vomiting once or in one place.

She would heave, we would instinctively spot it, dash to get her towel (or anything) before she would then produce the goods from her stomach. After which, she would move a few paces and, if the first lot wasn't on the carpet, you could almost guarantee she would move off the tiled floor and onto the carpet where she would produce seconds.

Over the years, we had gotten used to it and it was hers and our routine. This morning was different. There were more than two helpings and even more worryingly, there were 'accidents' happening on the carpet. The 'accidents' were coupled with *leakage.*

A word that is rarely positive. There was also blood from the 'non-meowing, or (in Marli's case), squeaking end'. The spots of blood were increasing in volume and places on the floor and Marli was clearly distressed. My wife had to go to work. Was I going to be expected to look after Marli?

Notwithstanding the vomit, 'accidents' and blood, I knew my wife would be worried to distraction, not just about Marli, but probably more so about whether I was capable of looking after her properly. I'd never been good with clearing up after, shall we say, 'incidences' and cleaning the litter tray was another job that was firmly assigned to the 'pink list'. We both knew the best course of action was not to leave her in my squeamish hands.

Me: "Call the vet."

Me: (In my head) *is this it? The moment? How will my wife get through this? How much will this cost?*

To be honest, the last two questions may have come in a different order. As my wife dialled the number, she was clearly worrying about Marli and her new responsibilities at work.

Wife: "I have to go to work, can you take her?"
Me: (In my head) *What if the vet gives me some choices? What if when I ring my wife, to tell her what's going on, I can't get through to her and I have to make a choice? What if the vet tells me the cost of being able to bring Marli home and my wife, shall we say, doesn't see my point of view?*
Me: "I think it's best if we both go. You'll have to call work and let them know."

The vet's response was, "bring her straight in," and so we knew she had to go. My wife made the relevant phone call to her boss, who was wholly supportive. Luckily, her boss had a horse and so understood the pet thing. If I'd been the boss, before having Marli, and before saying the right thing, I would have naturally thought, "Just get another one!"

Anyway, it was clear that my wife's boss understood and wholeheartedly felt that Marli had to go to the vet and that my wife should be the one to take her. With the appointment scheduled, we were on the way to the vet. My wife panicking, me worrying about my wife, Marli, the potential for a serious falling out between us and the aftermath of the whole scenario.

As you know, Marli was no spring chicken, but she did look good for an old girl and I was sure there were many more tunes to be played on this fiddle. Even so, every trip to the vet was stressful for us both, and for Marli even more so. The stress could be the deciding factor.

That being said, Marli seemed to somehow know we were going to the place to hopefully make her better and so, whereas before, any car journey spelt double trouble and catastrophic car sickness, her journeys to the vets now seemed to be taken in a more reserved lady-like way, during which she just sat quietly.

As we got to the vet, there were still instances of double trouble for Marli and a slight wait as there were other patients before us. Didn't they realise that our cat was the M.I.P (Most Important Patient) they were going to be having that day and should be seen immediately?

It wasn't too long before we were called and told, because of Covid restrictions, only one of us would be allowed in the examination room with her.

Me: *(In my head) What if my wife, just to make sure Marli is alright, agrees to a barrage of expensive tests and treatments which we have to pay for because they have already been done before I get a chance to interject?*

As they went in, I knew I had to trust the vet, my wife and myself to do the right thing and I hoped Marli would be fine and, in her annoying way, be sitting on our bed again in next to no time. The wait seemed longer than it actually was but finally, we were given the news.

Vet: "Marli has a case of cystitis (hence the blood and sickness) and there may be either crystals in her bladder that are making her ill or an infection. Anyway, we need to do some tests and she will need treatment."

As I looked at my wife's face, and her beaming smile, there was a clear sense that the drama was over, the issue had been diagnosed and that an agreeable treatment plan had been devised. I didn't ask how much it had cost and I still don't know.

What I do know however, is that the treatment they prescribed meant my wife now, twice a day, could hold Marli (as though she was a babe in arms) and, while using that annoying pet lovers voice, administer a series of medicines from a syringe type device, after which there was much cooing.

We hated it when Marli was ill, but, as they say 'every cloud—' because now my wife has the perfect excuse to treat her like, as my wife puts it, 'mummy's little baby'.

So coming back to:

Me: "Is that blood on the floor!"

I hope you can see why, when I saw the red patch on the bathroom mat, my heart, for several reasons, sank. Luckily, my heart lives to float for a while longer and more importantly, we still have a lodger on our bed.

While we'd been dealing with our feline dramas, the house build had continued, although all too often even though things were happening, it felt as though they were not, or that the builder had taken his foot off the gas.

When we were in the planning and design phase for the house, we thought we had thought of everything and all situations, how we were going to use the spaces, our ideas for the gardens, where the TV would be, etc.

In reality, there were lots of things that we hadn't really considered, such as where would the washing machine go? Where would we (or as it now was, I) do the ironing? Where would Marli's litter tray go? Even though we thought we had planned it all, it was only when things started to develop did we realise there were still, not only lots to be decided, but there were things that could change, and we felt we should take the opportunity to re-evaluate our ideas.

After all, if there were going to be changes, then now was the time to do them. Our builder on the other hand, at times, didn't quite see it like that. It was becoming clear that he thought we were the type of couple who couldn't make up their mind (he may have been right) and, or, expected him to make changes that would drastically impact on his original quotation for the job.

Five and a half months into the build, we were at the stage when we could see the full footprint of the house. We could walk around the shell of the building, pretending we were cooking, watching TV, or lazing by the pool, and it was at this stage the doubts, or as we liked to think of them, 'what ifs', started to creep in.

What if we built a wall here so we could do this or that, or changed our minds about where the washing machine, bathroom, dressing area, and several other things could be? What if we asked for a door here instead of there, or we asked the digger man to, while he was doing the jobs we had agreed on, he could just do a few other jobs, such as, moving soil from point A to point B so we could do things with the garden, or moving vast amounts of soil from under the house so we could have more storage space?

Storage space was something we had somehow neglected to consider during the design phase and, now we had the opportunity to do something about that, we didn't want to rue not doing something about it when we had the chance.

There were other things that fell into this category and, as I was on site every day discussing things with the builder, it became all too easy to suggest alterations, or what we considered to be slight amendments or bright ideas. The reality of the build being, for us, a process, and for the builder, a headache, was made very clear to us when our builder presented us with a quotation for all our bright ideas.

They came to 5% of the total budget for the build. The problem with ideas (especially the good ones) is that once you've had one, you couldn't, so to speak, put the toothpaste back in the tube, so we had to stump up the cash and accept the reality that we couldn't afford many more bright ideas. That said, the alterations we decided on, we thought were better, and so we hoped the extra money would be worth it. I'll let you know.

We obviously wanted the house to be built, finished, and like a shiny new pin, as quickly as possible. Therefore, until everything was finished, we wanted to see lots of workers on site, every day, all day. Our builder, although well established and experienced, had a small trusted team and frustratingly for us, other projects on the go.

That meant it was not always possible to flood the site with workers. To give credit where it was certainly due, the build was progressing well and I think it was because I was there nearly every day that it felt like the initial spurt seemed to have slowed.

My wife, because she was 'working full time', only got to the site at the weekends. She always seemed impressed by the progress, so I had to keep my impatience in check. After all, it was hopefully going to be 20 months from meeting our new architect to a finished build, and this was during the Covid pandemic. Compared to all the horror stories we were told at the start of our adventure, assuming everything continued to go to plan, we were doing well.

I'd made no secret of the fact that at the start, I wanted to be involved in the build at every step of the way and that I had my array of tools at the ready. I also still had my hard hat, but the chances of me ever wearing that were dwindling by the day.

So far, there had been very little for me to do. Until now. The chance came for me to dust off my tools and swing into action. The progress of the build had allowed us to begin to see our potential garden and we decided it would be nice to have some raised beds.

I had had days of watching the builders build things.

It didn't look that hard. Surely I could do that and furthermore, two birds with one stone; the possibility for a chance to go shopping for a new tool and to lay the groundwork to be able to proudly say to family and friends, "I built that!"

The builders had big trowels. Proper trowels, like the ones proper builders use. I had a diddy one, like the ones used by weekend DIY-ers. Being a child of the '70s and '80s, I was used to seeing my dad, rather than buying new, constantly fix things.

Nowadays, it seems like it's just easier, simpler, and more often than not, cheaper to 'get a new one', but back then, there was a culture of mending rather than replacing. I'd often see my dad struggle with whatever he was fixing, with the make do tool he was trying to use, and he would say, "You can't beat having the right tool for the job."

With his words ringing in my ear, if I was going to make a success of 'project raised beds' then one thing was definite. A new trowel was going to make all the difference. As I entered the store, I felt a strange macho glow. As I perused the number of different trowels, I felt a strange glow of ineptness.

Why are there so many different types of trowel? How was I supposed to know which one to get? Cue me handling the different trowels and pretending to do trowel things, while hoping no-one could see I obviously had no idea what I was doing. As I left the store, with my choice of trowel, I felt sure I had the right tool for 'a' job, but did I have the right tool for 'the' job? Only time would tell.

Fresh from our extras bill, I made sure the builder knew that I was going to be building the raised beds and so there was no need for him to consider them extras. This was his cue to make jokes about my proficiency as a builder and about whether I actually knew what I was doing.

Builder: Lots of jokes about whether I knew what I was doing. More jokes about whether I needed an engineer for my project.

Me: "YES. I know what I'm doing. NO. I don't need an engineer."

Builder: "Do you realise the foundations you have already put in are not straight?"

Me: "YES! They're supposed to be like that. They go with the contour of the land." (I'll leave you to decide.)

Builder: "OK then."

Me: "Obrigado."

As the builder left, with a chuckle and a smile, I began my assault on our patch of land that was to become, 'Our Raised Beds Area'.

When we were thinking about buying land and building a house, we had dreams of owning an expanse of land with room for animals, orchards and garden sculptures.

Now I had a shovel in my hand, and was digging, shovelling sand and gravel, moving blocks from pile A to make my own pile B, moving bags of cement in a wheelbarrow that had a flat tyre, and all under the beautiful Portuguese weather we had moved for, more than once, a particular question came to mind, 'Whose idea was it to move to Portugal, buy a big piece of land and build a house?' I wasn't worried though, I had a new trowel.

My weeks of watching the builders were put into action, with one difference. Things seemed to go right for them, and for me, nothing seemed to fit and everything was a struggle. My foundations were straight-ish. Straight-ish because wherever I started digging, I seemed to have the uncanny knack of finding solid rock.

Even when I decided to start in a new place because of a large rock I had found. Despite all the enthusiasm of digging in a new place, I just found another seam of rock. This meant the foundations were mostly flat, except where they weren't and, when this was coupled with the uneven ground, it was becoming abundantly clear that what was needed to solve my problems was know-how.

This realisation was quickly followed by, "Hmm! This isn't as easy as it looks." Perhaps unsurprisingly, my following thoughts, for the rest of the first day (and a half) were roughly exactly the same. I knew I had to pull myself together.

After all, raised beds don't build themselves and I had a builder and a wife to impress and an unimpressive pot of contingency money set aside for extras. I knew if we were going to have raised beds, then it was left to me to make beds that were raised. There was only one thing to do, go to YouTube.

Back in Blighty, we had done lots of projects with an equally unimpressive pot of money to do them with. An unimpressive pot of money usually meant that if things were going to get done, there would be no tradesmen or women, no crafts people, who actually knew what they were doing, and no coming home from work to find things finished.

On the contrary, an unimpressive pot of money usually meant embracing the phrase, 'if you want something doing, do it yourself' and we were no strangers to that. In our previous projects, we'd done lots of things for ourselves, including tearing down ceilings, knocking down interior walls, rebuilding walls, patio areas, an entrance from a garage to the main house (which actually passed a building's regulations inspection) and many other jobs.

To be honest, I can't say these jobs saved us either time or money, because they always took, if we were lucky, twice as long as they would have done if a professional would have done them, but they always provided us with:

a) some talking points; for example, when I decided to fit a front door myself and, 12 hours later, we still had no front door.

b) some serious fallings out, like when, irrespective of what was decided, my wife did what she always does, and did what she was going to do anyway, which by sheer coincidence, was the exact opposite of what we decided, and the very antithesis of what I would have done.

Despite all these trials and tribulations of BIY (Bodge it Yourself), the one thing our unimpressive pot of money had always given us was the chance to say, 'we did that'. So, with another opportunity to say, 'I did that', staring me in the face, I knew the time had come to own part of our build, roll up my sleeves and get stuck in.

In all the projects I'd done previously, I'd never encountered having to build walls on sloping ground and, although this was going to be the first of three beds all on sloping ground, this first one had to be right because it was closest to the house and so would be seen by anyone lucky enough to be near my raised bed, while at the same time being close enough to hear me say, "I did that."

I sought the advice of the builders on site, but for some reason, I quickly got the impression they thought I was just someone with too much time on my hands, and so, just to show them that although they may be right, they shouldn't be too quick to judge, I wanted to do it on my own (YouTube notwithstanding).

YouTube was great for passing the time of day. For all those times when you should be doing something constructive and you realise the next clip of banal, interesting, sporting, surprising, or forgotten video footage was only a click away and would only take 3 to 4 minutes to watch.

Three hours later, you've done nothing and, guess what, the next clip of banal, interesting, sporting, surprising, or forgotten video footage was only a click away and would only take 3 to 4 minutes to watch.

YouTube was also great for finding out how to do things, except in my case, typing, 'how to build a raised bed on sloping ground in a small hamlet in Portugal', surprisingly came up with few results and, although there were several guides and videos on how to build everything from walls to complete houses, what I needed, aka, a complete step by step instruction guide (with downloadable manual and person to come, completely free, and do the job for us), was not instantly popping up. So, I knew what I had to do. Wing it!

It's fair to say I didn't make the best job of the block work, made all too clear when one of the workers came over during his lunch break with a 'let's see what that guy's been up to' expression on his face and declared, "Ah, Rustico!"

It was also fair to say that building the beds was only half the job as in order to make them look nice, they had to be rendered in cement. Luckily, one of the workers, probably worried he was going to be asked to make my work look presentable, took pity on me and gave me a crash course in making the world's most untidy block work invisible.

Despite all that, with moments of self-doubt and the contemplation I may have to ask the builder to rescue me, four weeks and four pairs of gloves later, we were the proud owners of; a well-used builder's trowel, a wheelbarrow with a repaired tyre and, built in blocks and cement, complete with level edges, and rendered finish, three raised beds.

There had been:

a. Blood (when, in a misguided attempt to save money by not buying a new tyre), I fell over trying to wheel a barrow full of cement across our uneven ground (I bought a new tyre).

b. a lot of sweat (damn the Portuguese sunshine), but thankfully, and I'm happier than perhaps I should be to say, no tears (although I came close, when I realised I had to demolish 50% of what I'd done because I'd completely misjudged the slope and made one of the beds too high and another one too big).

Despite all this, when the job was finished, alongside my smugness and pride, it was possible that the best part of 'project raised beds' wasn't buying a new trowel, tyre, or solving the problems of uneven foundations and ground, or learning how to apply and finish cement render.

No, the best thing was seeing the builder's face when he realised all the jokes he had thought of, to be prepared for my failure, were never going to see the light of day. The job was finished and, if I say so myself, it looked pretty darn good (with a few original features) and, alongside all of that, forever and a day, I would be able to say, "I did that."

We had 'raised beds', I had new skills, my wife was 'working fulltime' and Marli was fine and still on our bed. What more could we ask for? I'll tell you. Answers. There were still the outstanding questions of what colour kitchen were we going to have? What showers were we going to buy?

Would I be able to turn the shower on before I got in it? (This was particularly important to me because every shower I've ever had, I've had to get in or reach inside to turn it on. I hate that first blast of cold water. It has never made sense to me why showers are like this and, if I was building a house this was going to be my opportunity to right some of the wrongs in life, so I was planning to make the days of the cold blast of water a thing of the past).

Where were the lights, sockets and switches going to go? Did we want a kitchen island or not? Does the outside kitchen need a sink and a fridge? Should we get an oven with Wi-Fi, a five or four ring hob?

How should we finish the patio? Where should the herb garden be? What tile should we use for the swimming pool? 65 inch or 75 inch TV? (See if you can guess which way I voted on that), should we change that brick wall for a glass door? Where should we put the avocado plants our landlady had been cultivating for us?

How could we build a house and, at the same time, solve the inequalities within the world? OK, not the last one, but it felt that although we had already made lots of decisions and answered lots of questions, we still had lots more of both to do.

Alongside this, it felt as though with every decision and answer, we had the, 'what if we make the wrong choices and everything looks rubbish' Sword of Damocles hanging over our heads (perhaps slightly melodramatic, but I think you get the point).

Things weren't all troublesome though. Given my penchant for all things retail, we did get to go shopping. For me at least (although I think my wife enjoyed it just as much) this was particularly exciting, made more so by the huge sigh of relief we were able to breathe as we managed to spend less than we thought we would have to on lights and light fittings.

All this excitement, and the rollercoaster that is building your own house, came with a stark reality check though. This period of the build was making one thing very clear and beyond doubt. We were slowly, but surely, entering the 'you do realise you can't change your mind and if you do, it is going to cost you a lot' phase.

Things were getting serious and we were getting excited.

What Cao Goes Woof?

The process of building a house was a long one and, if things went to plan, we would have lived in our rented accommodation for nearly two years. This brought with it its own issues. Our rented place was, without question, a nice place to be with a chilled and supportive landlady, a pool, and all the amenities we needed.

We also had a neighbour who had lots of dogs, but more about that later. Alongside some of the positives, it meant that my wife and I had been living in a 10m x 5m space in which we worked, cooked, relaxed and shimmied around all our belongings.

It also meant that our relationship and our ability to get along with each other with, the strains and stresses of building a house, had the potential to be severely tested. The Covid restrictions with the imposed lockdown, also meant that the things one previously took for granted, such as going for a meal or a local attraction, or doing things that helped to relieve the tensions of life generally, had not been available to us.

It was just me, my wife and Marli. The Covid years had also resulted in a total change in lifestyle for us both, with a re-evaluation of how much we worked and how much time we spent with each other. Despite all these challenges, I'm pleased to say our relationship seemed to have gotten stronger.

We were never a couple who had lots of arguments but, in our old life, every now and then, there would be something that niggled either one of us and this would result in not so much an argument but tension in our relationship or a harsh word or two. These flashpoints seemed to have disappeared and we just seemed to get along all the time (well, more than we did).

Now, our disagreements seemed to be about whether we should press the button in the car so we could have the top down as we drove. I liked to have it down as for me it represented our new life in the sun.

My wife, on the other hand, and probably more sensibly, preferred not, as the sun shining in just made things hotter and for her, less comfortable. We both used to work a lot and coupled with our big house (and the mortgage that came with it) we, in hindsight, had a lot on our plate.

Living in Portugal had changed all that and we were just happier. Of all the positives about our new country of residence, there had been one negative that one couldn't escape. Dogs.

The British are widely regarded as a nation of animal lovers and this is especially true when it comes to dogs. It has never ceased to amaze me how much the British love dogs and more than that, it has never ceased to amaze me how much British dog owners expect other people to love their dogs.

It is a constant annoyance to me that dog owners, and this is also true of the owners we encountered in Portugal (albeit mainly the British ones) took their dogs for walks but invariably not on a lead, meaning that when I am walking, cycling or trying to enjoy some outside time, I had to deal with a dirty smelly dog (OK, that may be a little harsh, but you get the point) coming near me.

I don't like dogs and the main reason is because they usually come with inconsiderate owners who, for some reason choose to ignore the reality that firstly, not all people like dogs, secondly, just because you own a dog that shouldn't mean other people have to be impacted by it, and thirdly, dogs have the potential to bite. This potential is not minimised just because the owner says, "Oh, he/she won't hurt you."

They don't know that. Dogs are dogs and they do what dogs do and one of the things dogs do is bite things and people. Yes, I accept that dogs can be loving creatures and a great comfort to their owners but they are not a great comfort to me and I don't want dogs near me.

My feeling is, I shouldn't have to deal with dogs and their potential to bite and generally be a pain. In my view, when out in public, all dogs should be muzzled and on a lead. If, when driving, we have to wear seatbelts, just in case of an accident, then why don't dog owners have to put their dogs in a muzzle and on a lead, just in case they revert to type and take a chunk out of me or anyone else.

The Portuguese word for dog is *Cao*, which is pronounced 'cow'. In many ways, the Portuguese view of dogs is similar to the Brits and their Portuguese owners here displayed the same inconsiderate approach as their British counterparts. However, there was one extra element that, if I was king of the world, it would be top of my list to fix. The Portuguese allowed their dogs to bark, *todo dia, todos dia* (all day, every day; as you can see, my Portuguese is getting better).

Our rented apartment was in a residential area and there was always a dog barking. In fact, if it was just one, it wouldn't be too bad, but it wasn't. It seemed like every Portuguese household had at least one dog and every Portuguese dog just barked all day and night with their Portuguese owner not seeming to get it that not everyone wanted to hear their dog barking.

This is especially true at night when there is, and this is without exaggeration, a chorus of all the neighbourhood dogs barking because all of the other dogs were barking and setting each other off. This brings me to our neighbour, who has eight dogs. Yes, eight.

He also has sheep, so one might expect him to use the dogs for the sheep but weirdly, he has more dogs than sheep. Why does anybody need eight dogs? Anyway, on top of this, he leaves the dogs outside day and night and yep you guessed it, they just bark, whine, make that high pitched sound that suggested they were deeply unhappy and possibly being mistreated or at least not being properly cared for and then barked some more.

In fact as I write this, I can hear his dogs, the dogs of neighbouring properties and the dogs down the road, all barking. Among other nationalities, it is a constant source of angry Facebook posts with many, it seemed, being driven to the precipice of madness, as their Portuguese idle is blighted by not only the barking of dogs but probably more so by the lack of consideration displayed by their owners who, despite complaints from their neighbours, didn't seem to see it as an issue.

Our landlady even went to the trouble of baking our (dog loving or shall we say dog keeping) neighbour a birthday cake and writing him a letter, in Portuguese, explaining that the constant barking was affecting the quality of her and her unwell partner's life.

At that time he had four dogs, so either my landlady was a terrible baker or he just doesn't seem to care or understand. To add a cherry to the top of the cake that is dog barking, the Portuguese often kept their dogs in their gardens, which meant as you took a minding your own business stroll along a country path, or residential street, you were scared half to death when a dog (but most likely two, three or four dogs) hurled itself at the garden fence, barking and snarling at you as though you were wearing a stripy top, complete with face mask and swag bag.

I'm not sure if I'll ever get used to the barking and luckily, where we are building our house is out in the sticks with no neighbours and more importantly, no dogs within earshot but, if you ever pick up a newspaper and see the headline *Man Bites Dog*, I guess you'll know how I'm getting on.

At the risk of dwelling on the negatives, there are many positives to living in Portugal and these definitely outweigh our canine critters. One of the positives is, Covid permitting, when living in Portugal you can do things that you would only normally do on holiday, so you feel like you are able to go on holiday whenever you want.

When we lived in England, the nearest beach or seaside resort was, if we were lucky with traffic, two hours' drive away. It was also cold, grey and whenever there was a sunny day, it would be packed with other people looking to enjoy the same small stretch of beach as us.

Where we were in Portugal, and where we would be, there were at least four beaches within a 20-30minute drive and over 300 sunny days. This meant you could go to the beach whenever you wanted and, except during high season when the beaches were full of British tourists, they were not overcrowded and you could usually find a quiet spot for a bit of R'n'R'n'R (Rest, Relaxation, Romance).

One such trip led to us trying something we had never done before and, because of the bone jangling temperature of the British waters, we were never likely to try in England. Paddle Boarding. So there we were, having driven for 20 minutes we were being given our first lesson on how to paddle board.

It seemed simple. All you had to do was get on the board in a kneeling position and start paddling and then, when you felt confident, you would stand up and that was that. My wife went first and she seemed to get the kneeling bit straight away.

In fact, although she swore differently, it looked to me as though she had done this before and could have quite happily and successfully auditioned to be one of the guys from the opening credits of the original Hawaii-Five-0.

Then it was my turn. After some pointers from our instructor, I got on the board quick enough.

The problem was, I seemed to have a natural ability to fall off even quicker and, as I moved further and further away from the shore, it kept happening. It then dawned on me that our Portuguese instructor had done something very Portuguese.

He had left out a vital piece of information. He had told me how to get on the board while I was near the shore, but he hadn't told me how to get back on the board when I was in the middle of the lake. My embarrassment, and my wife's amusement, then went to new levels as I floundered while trying to style things out. Further levels of female amusement were reached as the rescue boat was dispatched.

From my perspective, this was to save my wife from falling off her board because she was laughing so much. From a different perspective, the dispatching of the lifeboat may have been to save me from myself with the added bonus of reducing the need for the paddle board company to claim on their public liability insurance.

I was as buoyant as a brick and no matter how much I tried, and to my wife's amusement (spelt S.M.U.G.N.E.S.S), I just couldn't get the hang of it. So much so, I was on the verge of inventing a whole new pastime, *SWDCPD-ING* (Swimming While Desperately Clinging to a Paddle Board).

My ego was shot, my wife was better than me and I was on the cusp of trying to style out failing. Then, it happened, I was on, I stayed on, I paddled, I was doing it. Then I fell off again. This was the way of things for most of our paddle-boarding escapades, my wife laughing at me and me falling off the board.

At one point I even managed to stand up, which was more than my wife achieved (something I will treasure forever) but it wasn't long before there was the tsunami of me falling back into the water. On one such occasion, I fell in and when I bobbed back up, no doubt with a half drowned look and lots of spluttering, I realised I had lost my sunglasses.

In hindsight, this was probably the best part of the day because it meant I could play James Bond and, in true 007 fashion, I rushed to our car, took out my snorkelling gear, and proceeded to dive underwater to find my glasses.

As the familiar theme tune was being sung in my head (Der da der der), I searched for my glasses. I found them and the sense of achievement, as I held them aloft to by now what was the full theme tune, complete with orchestral backing (Der da der der da der der) was an unforgettable moment and, just so I could find them again, worth losing my glasses for.

As we got into our car, and had the usual top down or not debate, I pressed the button. On this occasion I won and, as I looked forward to the wind blowing through her hair and across my scalp, we took the long way home (25 minutes). We reflected on the day, the fun one of us had had and, before their heroic saving of the day, the trauma the other had had and the fact that our move to Portugal meant things like this could now be more than one-off holiday experiences.

We added the day to our developing list of why moving to Portugal was right for us and the list was further added to when we agreed that for us, on the whole, things in Portugal seemed not only more possible but more probable.

For me, I think the best thing is seeing and hearing my wife laugh more, usually at me, but nonetheless, the sometimes grey and tired look she used to have when we lived in England was nowhere to be seen; instead, there was a glow and an energy that was better to be around and be a part of.

Alongside this, in these summer months my wife wore less clothes than she used to. By that I mean she was either in one of her two swimming costumes, or wearing shorts and a

T-shirt and, despite how distracting this could be, it was another definite plus side to our move.

As each day passed, it was clear to us that there was nothing we missed about our old life. I thought there might be something I would pine for but there wasn't, and now there was even an English Tescos here, so English bacon and sausages were only a short drive away.

That being said, there was actually one thing that was missing from our new idle, a decent curry restaurant. Where we used to live in the UK, we were blessed. We had two outstanding places that were able to provide us with our sometimes twice-weekly curry fix and both had the ability to surprise, delight and provide just enough spice for an evening's entertainment.

In our new life, so far, we hadn't been able to find a similar quality and more importantly, authenticity in the curry restaurants we'd tried. Anyway, despite the obvious sacrifices and hardships, we were adamant that the search for our Algarvian curry Mecca would continue.

When we were planning our move, there were a few unknowns about how we, and Marli, would cope. Would we cope with the near constant good weather? Would we miss the 'four seasons in one day' phenomena that was England and would Marli cope with the drive here and her new surroundings?

Our concerns however, had never come to anything. We didn't miss England and (I better say this) unlike my wife, although Marli was beginning to show her age (she now limps at all four corners), if the cat shaped patch on the rug is anything to go by, she seemed to be enjoying her retirement in the sun.

Of an evening, she had even taken to asking for a garden stroll, during which, after my wife placed her on her harness and lead, she limped around for a few steps before relaxing by the pool. In fact, if she had a pair of sunglasses and a G & T in her paw, then the synergy between her and my wife would be complete.

I Thought Portugal Was Cheap

While our house build continued at a pace, within the last few months, things actually felt like they had slowed down. Until this point it had been easy to see daily, or at least weekly progress and, after nine months, the fundamental structures were in place.

The feeling that things had slowed down stemmed from the fact that after the structure or house shell is in place, and before fixtures and fittings, there were lots of jobs that needed to be done before we got to the stage we were both desperately waiting for. The finishing stage.

We still took great delight in visiting the site and making all the plans you would expect, such as measuring for furniture, and pretending to swim in our, at the moment, empty and untiled pool, but our frequent visits also meant that we didn't always see the actual progress that was being made.

It had not been helped by the fact that on some days, there had only been one or two workers on site and this remained a bone of contention with our builder. We understood he needed to balance his commitment to us and his commitment to his other clients but at times, it was difficult to stay patient.

In the larger scheme of things, we were extremely pleased with the builder we had and he was ahead of the initial schedule he gave us. However, from our perspective, if he had more workers on site, our dream could have been realised much quicker. On the plus side, we were now at the stage where we got to go shopping.

I've made no bones about the fact that I love shopping and that even includes doing the weekly shop, so I'd been looking forward to this stage for months. That said, now we were there, and as we browsed the shops, the internet and everything in between, the reality of building your own house kept rearing its ugly head.

Things were always more expensive than you thought they'd be, wanted them to be and it always seemed to be the case that the one you liked, and wanted to buy, was usually the most expensive option. One of the reasons we chose to move to Portugal was to re-calibrate our life and our expenditure.

Portugal has a very different economy to the UK and while in the majority of Portugal, things were undoubtedly less expensive, in the Algarve, as we were coming to realise, things were not as inexpensive as we initially thought. In the UK, we had good jobs that paid well but we also had lots of out-goings, so money went out as fast as it came in and in some cases faster.

In our last house, we spent a lot of money on everything we bought and without really thinking about it, usually going for the fancy option; the new cars with all the extras, one of which was a DVD player (that never saw one DVD disc), the oven with 40 different settings, even though we only ever used one or two.

The new shoes and clothes that were not needed and rarely worn, holidays that *were* needed, but were very costly, expensive meals in overrated restaurants that were rarely better than the meals we prepared at home and, the continual gripe between us, having to put the central heating on in what were supposed to be the summer months. We were both bored with the annual conversation that went something like this.

Me: "Have you put the heating on?"
Wife: "Yes, I had to."
Me: "Why? Its summer."
Wife: "It's raining, I need to dry the washing and I'm a bit chilly."
Me: "Put a jumper on!"
Wife: "I'm already wearing three layers!"
Me: "Make it four!"
Marli: "Squeak, squeak, squeak." (*Translation*) This rug is particularly comfortable, but any chance of a tummy rub just to sweeten things a little?

So, as we reached the shopping stage, we were keen to make sure we didn't spend over the odds for things and we were keen to resist the temptation to buy the fancy option just because it was the fancy option. We were also keen to make sure we stayed clear of the ET merchants who were used to dealing with those living in the Algarve who appeared to have moved here to enjoy a bling lifestyle, of which there were many.

Even so, the bills were starting to add up and this was on top of the extras we had asked the builder to do and the cost of all the things we never thought of when we decided to move and build a house. When we got our initial quote, it made clear that some things were not included. One of which was the kitchen and its installation.

They say (although I'm still not quite sure who *they* are), the kitchen is the heart of the home and our research suggested that there was a formula to work to when budgeting for a kitchen. The formula talks of 'no less than 5% and no more than 15% of the value of your home plus an extra 20%'. So with our research done, we did the maths.

Me: (In true Yorkshire style) "HOW MUCH? Is that with all appliances, a chef to do all of the cooking, a waitress to serve your meals and a washer upper to do the dishes?"

Wife: "Would you like to sit down?"

Me: "Yes, please. HOW MUCH? WHY DO KITCHENS COST SO MUCH? THEY ARE JUST BITS OF WOOD!"

We had said before embarking on the build that it would be wrong to compromise on the essentials, and we wanted to have a house we were going to be proud of, but after having had an expensive kitchen in our previous house, which for several reasons I think we both regretted buying and then resented paying for, we were keen to buy what was reasonable rather than once again getting drawn into buying what we thought we should buy.

With this thought firmly in our heads, we took a trip down the EN125. The EN125 is a road in the Algarve where, from tiles to toilets, doors to decorative designs and everything in between, the rich folk buy their stuff.

Our conversations with each shop (or boutique, which basically means they charge more) went something similar to the one above and as we received quote after quote (one of which included a hob for over 7000 euros) we were relieved when, for a whole kitchen, one quote came in at approximately the equivalent of two fancy hobs.

We were tempted, it was a very nice 'designer' kitchen, and it had these fancy things in the drawers where you could put your cling film and tin foil. It also came with some new-fangled finish that meant you could do all the things you would never do to your kitchen units, such as spill acid on them, or attack them with the world's sharpest knife and, with a simple wipe with a damp cloth, it would come up looking as good as new.

Then we realised the price didn't include measuring for the kitchen, delivering the kitchen, installing the kitchen, the appliances and the dreaded 23% IVA. After all that was factored in, I reverted to type and once again, in true Yorkshire fashion:

Me: "HOW MUCH? What, with NO appliances, chef, waitress and washer-upper?"
Wife: "Would you like to sit down?"
Me: "Yes, please."
Me: "HOW MUCH? WHY DO KITCHENS COST SO MUCH? THEY ARE JUST BITS OF WOOD!"

As we both looked at each other, we came to the most solid agreement we had ever come to since deciding to exchange vows at the altar. There was to be no acid in our kitchen, all knives were to remain just sharp enough for cooking purposes and our tin foil and cling film could just go in a drawer. We left the shop.

We were still intent on not making too many compromises and we were still going to build a house we would be proud of, but we are also not being drawn into thinking an expensive kitchen makes better meals. It doesn't.

With all of the house building programmes we had watched, articles we had read and research we had done, the one thing that seemed to be true of about 95% of people who embarked on building their own house was, they set a budget and a contingency and then proceeded to ignore both and spend more than they thought.

I wish I could say we were not in that group but unfortunately, we were. One of the challenges we faced had been managing the relationship between the builder, architect and budget, or as we liked to call it the *B.A.B*.

The builder had a way of doing things to ensure a good product at a profitable price, the architect had a conceptual idea that was at times more aligned to aesthetic principles rather than budgetary considerations and we had our tussle between wanting a fantastically designed and executed house build, with the benefit of the experiences from both parties, while at the same time wanting absolute value for money, with as much for as little as possible.

All of the extras had resulted in a more limited budget than we initially realised. We had a budget for the build, with a few shekels just in case the unexpected happened, that was supposed to be bolstered by a job I no longer had. We naively failed to include everything that was going to be needed.

I'm generally not in the habit of giving advice because, after all, what do I know? That said, I do know this, 'Things Cost More Than You Think', so to all budding self-builders, be careful to ensure your *B.A.B* balancing act doesn't include the word Bankruptcy!

With each passing month and as the build had progressed, as one stage was completed and the next one began, there was invariably a new team of workers, or new individuals to get to know. With each one, the thing that struck me most was just how hard they worked and how many hours they did.

They usually had a six day week with a start time of 07.45 and a finish time of 17.30, with an hour for lunch. On top of that, much of the build had taken place in the months between March and October. These were the hottest months in the Algarve, with temperatures on some days hitting 38 and 39 degrees C.

Regardless of this, they were exceeding their schedule and doing a damn fine job. What probably helped was their ability to be good to themselves. What hadn't gone unnoticed was their lunch boxes often contained a couple of beers, or a jam jar of wine, and on site barbecues were a regular occurrence.

In fact, on one particular day, I arrived on site to find one of the guys had actually brought a barbecue set with him, had laid a makeshift table, complete with a dressed salad, cutlery, glasses for wine, side plates with bread, condiments and napkins and, rather than plastering something or throwing cement somewhere, there he was, tending a barbecue with seasoned chicken wings he had prepared the night before.

When I suggested I should be charging him for the use of my property for his pop-up restaurant, complete with countryside views, or at least a corkage charge, well, let's just say his response didn't need any translation. On the flip side, lunch was delicious.

Alongside their culinary contribution, the builders had also become accustomed to 'Beer Friday', although one downside of having more men on site at times was that it was beginning to cost more and more in beer.

Nevertheless, at approximately 16:00 every Friday my blue van pulled up and you could almost feel the anticipation as I climbed out of my van, opened up the boot and produced our recently purchased cool box. As I went round each worker, handing them their weekly token of our appreciation for their hard work, it was not uncommon for some to break into song, or liken my arrival to a religious event.

It was particularly pleasing to me to see them all take just a five or ten minute break to enjoy a cold one and catch up on some small talk with each other before diligently returning to their various jobs.

I may be over-stating it, but I really do think it made a difference to their day, week and impression of me and it definitely made me feel good, knowing I was trying to do my bit to show them just how much we did appreciate their work.

One of the builders who, unbeknownst to me, was a Muslim didn't drink alcohol. On his first week on the job as I did my rounds, I produced a can of beer for him only for him to explain the situation. A week later as I did my weekly rounds, I felt I could see he thought I had forgotten him.

I reached into my cool box and, as I pulled out a can of that well known popular cola drink (which incidentally cost me about four times as much as each can of beer), the look of appreciation on his face and the recognition that I hadn't forgotten about him was worth the extra cost and had been worth the addition to the weekly 'Beer Friday' bill.

I liked to think that in life one generally got what one gave and so when it came to offering help and advice on my projects, the builders had been invaluable. Whether this could be attributed to 'Beer Friday' or not was up for question. It wasn't the purpose of introducing it and it wasn't the purpose of continuing it but I suspect it didn't harm things.

It also gave me an excuse for a cheeky beer on a Friday afternoon. Although drinking alone can be fun, it perhaps shouldn't be done too often and there was no harm in me sharing a communal moment with the guys.

Nonetheless, when called upon, for example during operation 'Raised Beds', they offered advice and guidance on everything from block laying to cement plastering, rendering, how to build on a slope and, as I asked them questions on how to do things, they were on hand to put up with my terrible, but slowly developing Portuguese.

I'd also learned from just watching. The biggest thing I'd probably learned was that they made mistakes too (but thankfully less than I did) so I shouldn't be too hard on myself when I got something wrong, like picked up the wrong end of a tool, put something in the wrong place or had to start again because the first time was a complete disaster.

Now that our budget was being severely tested and we were realising there were more than a few things we hadn't accounted for, the need for me to get stuck in was becoming more apparent. One such job that was going to cost more than the zero we had previously budgeted for it, was the fencing.

The land our house was being built on just looked like normal earth. That was until you tried to dig a hole, at which point you realise that it was full of rocks and big stones and bigger rocks and bigger stones.

Every attempt to get a shovel of earth invariably resulted in feeling like a character from a Bugs Bunny cartoon; as the shovel hit a rock and the only movement was the vibration of every single bone and sinew in your body and you looked down and saw what felt to be a rock smiling up at you.

The other thing we didn't really think about when we decided to buy a big piece of land, was that big pieces of land need a lot of fencing and fencing needs posts and posts need holes. Maybe my wife thought about it, as she realised she wouldn't be doing any digging but I, and not for the first time during our little escapade, never really put 2 and 2 together.

As the quotes came in for the fencing, and then the metal posts, I worked on my maths. It became clear that if there were ever going to be holes for those posts to go into, I was going to be digging them. So I planned for day one of 'Operation Fence Post Hole'.

I had my shovel, pick axe and like Dr King, I had a dream. It turned out, I needed these three things but I also needed some heavy duty digging equipment, because at the end of day one, all I had was blisters on my hands, a shovel that was more bent than before and an ache in my back that made me question not only whether this dream thing was actually worth it, but also made me question whether instead of a fence, we should just get an energetic dog that could keep running round the grounds.

The builders had seen my floundering attempts and after a quick word, surprise surprise, they had the very tool I needed. A proper big drilling machine. As day two arrived, I decided to take the day off. My back was killing me.

Fast forward a few days and there I was, with a new found zest, the same dream, a slightly better but definitely weaker back and a big brightly coloured piece of heavy machinery. What could go wrong?

When you watch self-builders on the telly, the guys using heavy machinery look glamorous and manly, as they wield their weapon upon some unsuspecting concrete and then, straight after the advert break, the job was finished and they were onto the next thing.

It may surprise you to know that in reality, it's not like that. It's bloody hard graft. Why do big drills have to be so bloody heavy? Why does rock have to be so hard and why is it that whenever you need a fence post hole digging fairy, there's never one around. Did I mention it was bloody hard graft?

Yes, there were kind words from my wife, which were nice and welcome, but they don't get holes dug. Men get holes dug and this man dug holes. I'm not sure whether I hated loving every minute of it or loved hating every minute of it but, as I pulled the drill from the last hole and as I felt my back question life, the universe and whether I was going to ever stand up straight again, several things were without doubt.

I knew we had holes for fence posts, I knew we had saved lots of money, I knew the whole 'in sickness and in health' thing that my wife had promised was going to be put to the test and finally, I knew I never wanted to see that drill again.

Marli in Portugal

Before I met my wife, she had Daisy. Daisy was a black cat with small patches of white fur under her chin and on her paws, a particularly pink nose and she was the love of my wife's life. Daisy knew this and she was regularly spoiled with treats and hugs and, I suspect, kisses (although my wife denies the kissing bit because she knows I hate the idea of kissing animals).

Daisy had seen my wife through her good times and her not so good times and had been there for her whenever my wife needed to care for something, or needed something that would always respect her love.

Daisy was allowed to sit anywhere in the house, to go into the bedroom and to sleep on the bed. She was an indoor cat and so never travelled further than the garden gate and Daisy was everything my wife needed and wanted.

Cue the arrival of a tall dark handsome stranger (I'm sure you recognise the description), whose then object of lust, meets, and falls head over heels in love with. My wife is, and was a lady so obviously, I wasn't immediately invited to her house.

We got to know each other during various dates, days out and work events and during all of these getting to know you sessions, my object of lust would occasionally talk about her cat and I would occasionally make it clear that I didn't have pets, never really had them as a child (we had a budgie that died and a dog that ran off) and wasn't really into having animals in my house.

Anyway, as we became more than friends and colleagues, I became a regular visitor to her house and had to come to terms with just how important Daisy was to my wife. At this stage in our relationship I didn't get it, but my object of lust had become much more than that and so I had to accept that the package included Daisy.

By this stage, Daisy was approximately 18 years old and, as I now know, that was a serious age for a cat so I thought it wouldn't be too long before she was out and I was well and truly in. It didn't quite turn out like that.

Before me, Daisy had my wife all to herself. Now I was on the scene, much to both mine and Daisy's dismay, Daisy had to share my wife. There were only ever two things me and Daisy would come to agree on. The first was, neither of us liked or wanted to share my wife and the second thing we agreed on was that chicken is very tasty.

My wife had been vegetarian for years and so Daisy never got real meat coming into the house. Now I was about, there were regular helpings of chicken to be had. Apart from that I think we tolerated each other for the sake of my wife, the person in the middle. I constantly got the feeling that Daisy would look at me as if to say one of two things, either:

"So you're the reason I can no longer sleep on the bed."
Or
"Besides the chicken thing, what good are you?"

Even though my wife would try to reassure me that in actual fact, Daisy was my second most enthusiastic supporter, I think the three of us knew the truth.

Daisy became 19 years old, then 20, 21, 22 and all the while I got the same two looks. When Daisy turned 23, for much of that year, she remained as healthy as a chicken-loving cat. Then suddenly, she became ill. Then quite quickly after that she became very ill and then quickly after that, my wife made the decision to let Daisy rest in peace.

My wife was distraught with grief and I had never seen anything like it. To me, she was just a cat. I was sad my wife was sad, but surely there was no need to go overboard. I didn't get it, I also didn't provide the understanding and support she needed and I think it was fair to say my wife didn't really appreciate my point of view and there were probably moments when she questioned whether tall dark handsome strangers were all they're cracked up to be.

During the days after Daisy, my wife struggled to get past it and I struggled to get it at all. At one point, I even think we had a row because she was still prone to crying for her loss, and I was still prone to saying things like:

"What's for dinner?"
Or
"It was only a cat."

I remember thinking at the time, if losing a pet was that traumatic then why have one. I also remember thinking, I'm not sure I could go through that again, so I made an executive decision. There were to be no more cats for us. From now on, it was just going to be us two and no fur.

As the months passed, my wife's grief became more controllable and we managed to find an even keel and, so that my wife had something other than me to look after, we even bought some fish, complete with a fancy fish tank and fish tank things for fishes.

Every now and then my wife would say things like:

Wife: "Do you know, I don't want another cat because Daisy was so special, but if I did have another one, I'd like a tabby cat."

I would then immediately say something like:

Me: "We are not having another cat. We have fish."

This went on for a year or so and I thought we had finally laid to rest the desire to have fur everywhere, a litter tray that needed emptying and vet bills. In fact we had laid it to rest, we were never going to get another cat.

A Rainy Night In Autumn

So there I was, minding my own business, driving home from work when my phone rang. It was my wife.

Me: (*Hands-free, of course!*) "Hello, darling (or something equally loving), I'll be home soon."
Wife: "You'll never believe what's just happened."
Me: "What? Are you ok?"
Wife: "As I was driving home, I thought I saw something in the leaves by the side of the road."

Me: "What do you mean you saw something?" (My wife has a way of making every story heavy on narrative but sketchy on details.)

Wife: "I don't know, I just had this gut feeling and so I parked the car at home and walked back to where I saw it."

Me: "You did what? It's dark out, anything could have happened, you could have been attacked or anything. Are you mad?"

Wife: "I've found a little tabby kitten next to the road. It looks like it's only a few months old but it's been injured, I think a car must have hit it or something. I couldn't leave it there so I've brought it home. Can you buy some cat food and litter on your way home?"

Me: "What? A cat? How do you know it doesn't have fleas or something? You've taken it into the house? What are you going to do with it?"

Wife: "Just get here as soon as you can."

As I arrived home, I thrust the cat food into my wife's hands and she looked up at me.

Wife: "Ah, you've bought luxury cat food. You big softie."

That evening, we proceeded to care for the cat and as we phoned the RSPCA there was a definite mantra going through my head. I'm also pretty sure I said it out loud a few times.

Me: "Well, we can't keep it."

Now, as I think back, there was a somewhat unusual and strange silence from my wife. Anyway, our calls to the RSPCA were successful and we took the cat to them so they could look after it.

After a few days, my wife made a call 'just to see how the cat was getting on', and we were told she had suffered a broken pelvis (hence her sunshine reggae walk I told you about earlier) had had an operation and was now being cared for by a foster carer until a new home was found for her.

Me: "Excellent, we've done our bit, the cat's fine and eventually, it will find a new home."
Wife: "Can we go and see her at the foster home?"
Me: "Why? What for? What's the point? We are not having her. I thought you said you didn't want another cat."
Wife: "I don't, I just want to see that she is alright."

A few days later and as we pulled up outside the foster home, I'm pretty sure I said something like:

Me: "Don't bother getting attached, we are not having another cat."
Wife: "Don't worry, I just want to see her."

Just before we knocked on the door of the cat foster home, I gave my wife my 'I'm being serious' stare. The door was opened by your quintessential old woman, except this old woman had way too many cats. So much so that as the door opened, you were immediately engulfed by the smell of cat urine to the point it made your eyes water.

Smelly Cat Lady: "Oh, hello. You must be the people the RSPCA told me about. They said you would be coming. Come in."

Me to my Wife: "DO NOT TOUCH A THING IN HERE. ONE LOOK TO SEE THE CAT IS ALRIGHT AND WE ARE LEAVING."

The house was disgusting, dirty, smelly, full of cats and no doubt other less noticeable creatures, and as we saw the tabby kitten in her cage-like box, we both knew we couldn't leave her there.

A Few Days And A Few Phone Calls Later

We were now the proud owners of Marli, our very own tabby kitten. Call it fate, call it luck, call it my wife's cunning ploy, call it what you want but the joy on my wife's face was real and she was rather cute. Marli was cute too.

There began my wife's love affair and my love-hate relationship with Marli, named after Bob, of course. As Marli grew, she gave joy and plenty of smiles to both of us. She was a pretty cat and I'm not just saying that. If you haven't already gathered, I'm not big on cats so one cat looked like another to me, but Marli was different.

She was a good-looking cat. She was energetic, lively and (probably because of her pelvis) rubbish at jumping. We used to watch her getting herself ready to make a leap and it was as if she was doing the mathematical calculations before she would leap, and just about make it.

I suspect that during her calculations, she always forgot to 'carry the one'. If math was not her forte then maybe catching birds would be? It wasn't. So what exactly would Marli excel in? There were two things she became brilliant at. Firstly, making my life better, because she made my wife's life better and secondly, the ability to show that she was my wife's cat more than mine. What do I mean by this?

One example would be when she would sit in our garden hoping to catch some rural rodent. She would sit for hours just staring at a section of the fence, as if watching Mouse TV, waiting for her victim. If she did manage to catch something, which she actually did on a few occasions, she would run right past me and proceed to present her offering, with a triumphant squeak, at the feet of my wife.

Why did she never think to offer me anything? To give another example, my wife and I have always been a two-car family and without routine, depending on what we were doing that day, we would each drive the big car or the small car.

Regardless of which car I drove, whenever I arrived home, Marli was nowhere to be seen. On the other hand, when my wife arrived home, and again regardless of which car she was in, there Marli would be, squeaking and saying, "Hello mummy, have you had a good day? I've missed you. I think it's time for cuddles, isn't it?"

How did she know who was in which car? Even if I had been with her all day, as soon as my wife arrived home, Marli would suddenly forget all about me and our special times together and would rush straight over to welcome my wife.

In the early days, she would come into our bedroom, as if she had some special backstage pass and, after completing a few miscalculated jumps, there she would be with her VIP viewing access to our private parlour games. I of course was outraged, my wife's reaction was perhaps unsurprisingly different.

Wife: "Ah. She just wants to be with us as a family."

My wife always took Marli's side when it came to disagreements so for example, when Marli climbed on the table, which I didn't like, my wife's response was never, "Marli, get off the table."

It would always be, "Ah, she just wants to be close to you. At the same level as you."

Or when I would kick one of the numerous water bowls that were scattered around our house, I would say something like:

Me: "That bloody cat."
Wife: "Marli never knocks them over."

I've always resented the fact that we couldn't just go away for the weekend or on holiday because we had to plan for Marli. We took her to a cattery once and when we picked her up, she hissed at the cattery owner. I had never heard her hiss at anyone, before or since, that wasn't her nature.

What had been going on in our absence? Neither we nor Marli ever went to that place again. This meant whenever we went away, we had to have a cat-sitter come into our house to look after her. I suggested that we teach Marli to read and then have seven food bowls, each with a day of the week written on so she would know what to eat and when.

For some reason, and despite having had Marli for 18 years, and with 18 modifications to the initial idea, it has never been approved at a higher management level.

So there we were, having had Marli for 18 years and now she was enjoying her retirement in sunny Portugal, with my wife still making excuses for her and me sneaking in cuddles late at night. After all, I do have a reputation to maintain.

Although Marli was comfortably in her retirement, she was often called upon for her 'Solomon-like' wisdom and to settle important decisions. One such occasion was when we had to decide if we were going to have an open fire (something I've always wanted) or a log burner (something my wife wanted).

For some reason, Marli had always loved sitting on sheets of paper and there had been times when our living room floor was decorated with single sheets of A4 so that Marli could nestle down in complete comfort. We decided to use her little kink for our own purposes and so we wrote the two options on separate pieces of paper and waited until Marli decided it was time for a little sit down.

True to form, the time came for Marli to rest her little legs and so we waited with bated breath to see which piece of paper was going to be that day's throne. Open fire or log burner. Log burner? or open fire?

At one point it seemed, just to tease us and inflate her own importance, Marli knew exactly what we and she were doing as she swayed from one option to the other. Then finally, her vote was cast.

Me: "That's my girl, well done!"
Wife: "Traitor! I clean your litter tray."
Me: "Would you like some tuna?"
Marli: "Squeak, meow."
Wife: "Don't even joke about it."

I always knew Marli was some kind of cat genius and now we had proof.

Then One Day...

Wife: "Marli hasn't really eaten for a few days and she seems, well, not quite herself."

Me: "She's fine, you know the rules, no vet bills."

Wife: "I think we just better monitor her for a few days."

That Night...

As my wife went to bed at her usual incredibly early time (my wife can sleep for England), she gave me strict instructions to keep an eye on Marli and wake her up if anything seemed untoward. I did as I was told and truth be told, Marli was not her normal self.

So much so that even I noticed it and became slightly worried, and not just about the vet bills. She seemed to be lacking in energy, was just huddled in the corner of the room and quite frankly, she looked really sad. Marli was unwell.

The Next Morning...

There was no change in her condition and so, after a call to the vet, we made an appointment and took her in. My wife was strangely calm at this stage and as we drove to the vet, our chat concentrated on where, in the new house, we were going to put Marli's litter tray.

At The Vet's...

The vet gave her the once over and ordered the relevant tests. During her examination, Marli remained listless. I could see that my wife was trying to be stoic, but I could also see her quivering lips. I was trying to tell myself that this would be just another vet bill and a drive home with our cat.

The Vet Gave Her Verdict...

Marli had an issue with her heart that needed specialist care, which could only be accessed the following day. In the meantime, she was given medicine aimed at regulating her heart rate in the hope that whatever the issue was, it had been caught early enough so it could be treated. She also had to stay overnight. As we said our goodbyes, the vet reminded us that Marli was no spring chicken. She was an 18-year-old cat.

The Next Day...

My wife's phone rang and it was the vet. The test results were in and the specialist had done an examination. We jumped in the car and within 25mins, we had arrived at the vet's surgery.

The Covid restrictions meant that only one of us could go in and so, as my wife steeled herself and I gave reassuring messages of hope, I sat in the car and waited for the usual good and bad news. Bad news, you have another vet bill; good news, Marli is coming home with you.

30 Minutes Later...

My phone rang. It was my wife. She was crying. "Can you come in please?"

I immediately thought, she's asking me to come in so she could tell me why we had to spend a lot of money. As I got into the examination room (after sneaking past the receptionist), my heart sank.

My wife was in tears and had Marli in her arms. The vet had a look of resignation on her face. Marli looked up at me. I could see she still had a twinkle in her eyes, but it was clear things were not right.

The test results had shown that time had indeed caught up with Mari and although, if we wanted to, we could take her home, there were no guarantees. She was unwell, hadn't eaten all night and would not get better. I wanted the cat we had had for the last 18 years, but sometimes you just don't get what you want.

Me: "Isn't there anything more you can do?"

Vet: "No. It wouldn't be fair and it probably wouldn't work."

Me: "Are you sure?"

Wife: "We love you, Marli. You have given us the best 18 years and we were so lucky to find you."

As my wife's tears continued to roll down her cheeks, the sadness on my wife's face was something I'd never seen before, and something I couldn't help with.

Wife: "We love you, Marli."

Me: "Thank you, Marli, for bringing me and my wife such fun. Now look what you've made me do."

I was crying. Just as I'm doing now as I'm writing this (luckily, my wife's not here). I tried to hold it in and be strong for my wife, but I'd never felt anything like it before. I'm not one of those guys who cries. I'm a traditionalist so I struggle with the concept of men crying in public.

For me, crying (especially if you're a bloke) is like farting, in that, wherever possible it should be done in private. I'd been with my wife for 26 years and she had never seen me cry before and now, this bloody cat was taking me to a whole new level.

I held Marli and she snuggled in the crook of my arm. She only ever did that with me. No-one else. Just me. I passed her back to my wife. The vet came from behind her examination table. We both stroked her.

Us to Vet: "Thank you for everything you've done."

After the vet had finished, we both, for the last time, sat with our little Marli.

Marli with the collapsible legs, our cat who had a funny, but cool walk, who loved tummy rubs, the crook of my arm, sitting on paper and helping to make the bed. Marli, who could never really meow properly and so just squeaked.

Marli, who did things I didn't want her to do. Marli, who used to get travel sickness (from both ends!) when driving 3 miles to the vet who then set out with two hapless idiots (OK, one) on a road trip to a new life in Portugal and who made the journey without so much as a 'are we there yet?'

Marli, who, on a cold rainy night in autumn was stranded, injured and left for dead and who changed our lives forever. Marli, who (let's face it, I don't like cats or animals) made me tolerate her, then like her, then love her. Marli, who gave my wife so much joy and allowed us both to share something very special.

I think my show of emotion shocked my wife. It certainly shocked me. In hindsight, although we both knew this day would come, I think we were both scared of what each other's reaction would be. I was scared that my wife would be inconsolable and I wouldn't be able to do anything about it.

On top of that, I was also scared she would be disappointed in me, and potentially a little angry, for not feeling the same as her. I suspect she was scared that she would be inconsolable and be faced with having to deal with my lack of reaction or lack of understanding.

Now the day had arrived, we were both taken aback and even though I think my wife had prepared herself for it, I certainly wasn't ready for it and neither of us were ready for my reaction.

When reflecting about that day, for some strange reason I think my reaction helped my wife, or at least I like to think it did. I think my show of emotion helped us both share something deeply saddening, at the same time, in a way that showed we understood each other.

We drove home in complete silence and as we arrived back to our rented accommodation, the overwhelming feelings were ones of sadness and loss. For me, there was also a feeling of togetherness.

For 18 years, we had been a team of three, now we were a team of two again (we were also 600 euros worse off. Bloody vet bills!). More importantly, we both knew we had been lucky enough to have had, not 'a' cat but to have had *Marli 'the' cat.*

AM in Portugal

The weeks *After Marli* (AM) were strange. We both missed her but never really talked about it. I'm not sure if it was because we had so many things going on, or because we didn't want to start each other off, but every now and again something would happen, or we would see something on the TV, and without saying a word, we knew how each other felt.

My wife said she was glad I was there for it and that I was able to support her through it. That was also my overriding feeling as it was my opportunity to show her just how much I had changed and how much it had affected me. We both still missed her and probably always would but we had to move on.

Covid had resulted in me being in Portugal for nearly 2 years without returning to the UK. That was never the plan, but to be honest, there wasn't much I'd missed about our old life. For many people around the world, Covid brought with it misery, personal and family loss and nothing but negativity.

It was clear to see that Covid was a leveller and it had levelled many and its legacy is yet to be felt and understood. Alongside the obvious heartache, it seemed like everyone we came into contact with was climbing the walls with having to spend time with their other halves and families and all the social media platforms were full of jokes and sketches about the pain of family life under lockdown.

I could honestly say, I was loving it. My wife and I were spending more time together than we ever had and it was more than good. It was great. So good in fact, I was dreading lockdown ending. Dreading feeling obliged to go to events I didn't want to go to, or having to shake hands with people.

Dreading having people, even though I'd just met them, feel they could give me a hug and invade my personal space, and even worse, having to look friendly when people go in or a kiss on the cheek or expect me to give them one.

I know it sounds grumpy but lockdown meant it could be how I liked it, just me, my wife and our life. Yes, we couldn't go to restaurants, or social events and as musicians, there were definite downsides to the lockdown and yes, we both had family we hadn't seen for months, but on the flipside, for us it meant we could save money, pour all that into the build and just enjoy each other without the input or interference of others.

Portugal had received international recognition for how it had dealt with the crisis and while we were here, all we saw on British TV was how badly the UK government had handled things, how the UK had the highest infection and death rate and, while in Portugal face masks were now the norm, in the UK, we saw pictures of crowds of people without masks.

Needless to say, we felt we had come to Portugal at the right time and we were glad to be where we were. That said, the time came when lockdown began to ease and I could no longer use the excuse of not being able to fly.

There was family to see and a few loose ends to tie up so, even though I was not looking forward to it, I planned a trip back to Blighty. As my wife drove me to the airport, all I was thinking of was returning back to Portugal. Strangely, travelling to England didn't bring with it a sense of returning home.

Instead, there was a sense of not wanting to leave home. We had both come to realise that our future was in Portugal or at least, our future was not going to be in the UK and, as we arrived at Faro airport, we commented on just one example of why we felt the way we did.

In England, when dropping passengers off, irrespective of how long you stay, every airport levies a charge. If you want to use a trolley for your luggage, you are met with another charge. In Portugal, it was free to drop passengers off and free to use luggage trolleys.

I've never really understood economics, but why is England so damned expensive? Why do British airports charge you for the privilege of dropping off or picking up passengers, or for using luggage trolleys?

Why is it that in the UK, everything seems to cost so much more, without providing much more. Why is it that in some parts of the UK, there are parking bays that collect more per hour than some people earn?

Before this turns into a rant, I think it is safe to say I knew that as soon as I touched down in the UK I was going to become reacquainted with my inner Yorkshire man, and the phrase 'how much?', was never going to be far from my lips.

I hadn't seen my family while I was in Portugal so my trip back to England was a chance to catch up with all that had been happening. I'm from a fairly large family with two brothers and two sisters, and each had had children, so I have an abundance of nieces and nephews.

Although my siblings and I are probably not emotionally close, in that we don't see or speak to each other very often, I like to think that when push comes to shove, we are there for each other. My parents had a stable, if sometimes, troubled marriage and, despite their ups and downs, had successfully raised 5 children without any being the subject of an episode of *Crime Watch* (a British TV series that featured unsolved crimes and appealed to the public for help in solving them).

Moreover, I'd say my parents had done a damn good job and all of my siblings had gone on to have successful careers in their chosen fields. My parents were married in 1966 and remained so. Sadly, during the time I'd been in Portugal, at the age of 79, my dad passed away and, due to Covid restrictions, I wasn't able to be with my family during his final days or at his funeral.

My dad and I didn't always see eye to eye and there were definitely times when I didn't understand where he was coming from. He was a proud, stubborn man, and there were times when he was an unpleasant man, but throughout, he was a hardworking man who always, and most probably at a sacrifice to himself, provided for his family.

In fact more than that, I can't remember a time when me or my siblings needed or wanted something that we didn't get. He always supported and encouraged our dreams (however fanciful), with the touch of pragmatism every childhood dream needed to be realised.

He also instilled values that I will forever hold dear. I do wish I had had the chance to ask him about the things we didn't agree on, but in reality, rather than providing any answers, it would have probably just ended up in an almighty row in which we both showed why we didn't see eye to eye.

He was my dad. A dad who, because of his Jamaican heritage and upbringing, had some great sayings, each of which would be prefaced by 'Ol time people always seh'. He would then proceed to encapsulate life and teach you a valuable lesson all at the same time.

He seemed to be able to fix anything with an engine, loved to dance, or as he put it, 'shake a leg', and he taught me to value who and what I am, without that value being dependent on others. I see many elements of him in me and without a doubt, he had left an indelible mark on me and how I, with my wife, live my life.

My mum is the typical matriarch figure every good home needs. Always there for her children, could give you a look that made you feel like you had just turned 10 years old and were a seriously naughty boy who was in need of, and would get, a good spanking and, in all but the most extreme circumstances, would always side with and protect her babies.

My mum, again probably due to her Jamaican-ness, also had a wicked sense of humour that had the dual ability to cut straight to the chase and reduce a room to either laughter and/or despair in equal measures. The fact that both my parents came from Jamaica, a country in which people would tell you the truth without feeling the need to perhaps soften the blow and the fact I was raised in Yorkshire, an equally forthright county, perhaps gives a hint as to why I am sometimes considered to be shall we say, direct?

Anyway, I like to think everybody knows where they stand with me and that what I say rarely needs interpretation. I also wish more people were like that. I hadn't told my mum I was coming to England so I hoped it would be a nice surprise for her.

One of my sisters picked me up at the airport, in her new Range Rover, wouldn't you know! It was so good to see her looking happy, confident and so damned rich, but again, it was a symbol of what my parents had instilled in us in terms of working hard.

It also gave me a clue as to who might be able to lend me a few quid if things went south down Portugal way. She had arrived at the airport a few minutes before I landed and it had cost her nearly £10 to pick me up. Told you England was expensive.

As we drove, to Mum's house, we caught up and I heard about my niece and nephew, both of whom were doing really well in their respective lives, with one, aged 20, buying a house and the other aged 18, basking in his successful A-level results and plans to study intelligent things at university.

After nearly two years of not seeing my mum, and after all that had happened, finally seeing her was more emotional than I thought it would be. There were tears, followed by much laughter.

This was quickly followed by my about to be a homeowner niece informing me that I had more grey hair and that I had put on weight. If you're lucky, the best and worst thing about family is honesty and within an hour of being back in the bosom that is family life, I was feeling lucky and unlucky in nearly equal measures.

My trip back also gave me the chance to see my other sister who is just the life and soul of any party. Again, she saw fit to share her honesty, but perhaps because of her experience and social etiquette, she also added how happy I looked. She was probably right on both counts.

I digress, but why is it OK to tell guys they've put weight on but seen as the height of rudeness to tell women the same thing? Anyway, I had a great time catching up with my folks and we shared the jokes and banter that only comes from being a family. Priceless.

I didn't get to see my brothers because neither live near my mum or sisters, but that was perhaps a blessing because in terms of honesty, when we get together, it's gloves off and every man for himself. I usually give as good as I get but as we musicians always say, 'you're only as good as your last gig'.

I had planned that I would spend some time with my family but also spend some time with myself and my loose ends. I'd left England two years previously, in a hurry, and thinking it wouldn't be too long before I returned, so there were things I needed to sort out at the rental property we had back in the UK.

So there I was, with some time to kill. I'd done all the tying up of loose ends and there was only one thing to do. Sit back, relax, enjoy the pop of a cork, and watch reruns of 'housey' type programmes. For most of them, I was probably watching them for the third time, but seeing all those couples coping with the stress of building came with a slight feeling of achievement.

We were doing what we had set out to do after being inspired by them, only our build was going swimmingly well, if a little slowly for our liking. We hadn't had all the dramas, the unforeseen problems, which brought extra costs or the inevitable delays that seemed to be a hallmark of every episode of every series of every programme.

That said, what did occur to me, was just how much fashions, trends, and more importantly, we had changed since we started on this journey. What were once our dream homes, with all the fancy gadgets, new building technologies, tightrope finances, and grey and white colour schemes, were now houses that seemed to ignore the art of simplicity.

We couldn't afford what they had and had been forced down the road of what was necessary. While watching, rather than previously feeling, 'if only we had more money', I was actually glad our limited finances had dictated our build.

We hadn't splurged on flashing lights, integrated sound systems, one touch controls for everything with a plug, or any of the all singing and dancing extras that seemed to be a must for all who went before us.

Instead, our time living in rented accommodation, which consisted of one room, a bedroom and a couple of bathrooms, had allowed us to realise, if we had built what we thought we wanted, we wouldn't be getting the house we needed.

One thing we could afford was the grey and white colour scheme, but even now that seemed like we were missing an opportunity to do the house we wanted rather than the house we thought we should have, so I was determined to go back to Portugal (or should I say home), with a new found confidence that we were doing the right thing for us and that we had to be a little more brave when it came to making our choices.

As I was enjoying my down time and new found bravery, I decided to give my wife a call so I could tell her just how brave I thought we should be.

Me: "Hi, I was just thinking about you. I've been *really* busy. Rushed off my feet. I haven't had a moment to myself." (I thought I'd lay it on a bit thick.)

Wife: "WE'VE HAD A FLOOD! There's water everywhere, everything is soaking wet and we are up to 3 or 4 inches in water. I and the landlady are having to move everything. It's a mess!"

My first thought was 'sounds bad'. This was very quickly followed by 'I'm glad I'm not there and I'm glad I'm not dealing with it'. Then for some reason, I thought, 'why did she say inches, when we had been metric for years and we were taught centimetres at school?'

Me: "Sounds like you've got better things to be doing than talking to me. Call me back when you can. Good luck. Love you!"

I knew it would have been better if I had been there, and I did feel a little guilty for being glad I wasn't, but other than literally shouldering the responsibility for lifting heavy things, what could I have done that they couldn't do.

They had managed to find the stop-cock and so the water had been turned off. I'm all for equality, as was my landlady, so this was an opportunity for the sisterhood to unite in a common struggle.

30 minutes later (and after a few sips of wine and more 'housey' TV).

Me: "Just thought I'd phone to see how you are getting on."

Wife: "It's chaos."

Me: "What's been damaged? Are my drum kits damaged? What about the paintings? Have you done this, that, the other? Make sure you (then came a list of things that, in hindsight, probably didn't help the stress of the situation)."

Wife: "We're doing the best we can, but because everything is so wet, it's all really heavy. We could do with some help."

Me: "I'll make some calls."

Despite the fact I was engaged in vital background fieldwork (sitting on the sofa, sipping a glass of red and watching 'housey' programmes) I leaped into action. I set up a remote operations room from which I could oversee our Iberian territories (put my drink down), sent out intelligence-based communications to my field agents (dialled two phone numbers) and I began to manage the situation. Then it hit me.

This was just like the film *Pulp Fiction*, where Vincent Vega (played by John Travolta), and Jules Winnfield (played by Samuel L. Jackson) accidentally shoot Marvin (played by Phil LaMarr), in the face. Vincent and Jules now find themselves in a pickle and call their line manager, Marsellus Wallace (played by Ving Rhames), and ask for his assistance in sorting out the chaos that ensued.

Now when I say, 'just like' I really mean 'something like', OK, 'tenuously like', OK, 'very little' like, but this was my chance to manage the situation and save the day.

In the movie, Jules makes the call to Marsellus Wallace and firstly, in a rather panicked state, explains the situation.

He then tells Marsellus, based on his and Vincent's predicament, what he would like to hear, by way of reassurance, from his line manager.

Marsellus duly steps up and provides the requisite assurances that he is handling the situation and he is in fact sending his top man, 'The Wolf' (played by Harvey Keitel) to take care of things. On hearing that Marsellus is sending *The Wolf*, Jules is immediately calmed and reassured in the knowledge that management is going to take care of things.

In my mind, and for the purposes of dramatic licence, my wife was playing the role of Jules, my landlady the role of Vincent and I, of course, was Marsellus. I just needed one more protagonist to play the role of *The Wolf*.

It went something like this, and... ***Action.***

Wife: "It's chaos."

Me: "What's been damaged? Are my drum kits damaged? What about the paintings? Have you done this, that, the other? Make sure you—"

Wife: "We're doing the best we can, but because everything is so wet, it's all really heavy. We could do with some help."

Me: "Don't worry, chill out, I'll sort it."

2 minutes and 24 seconds later (ish)
I called my wife.

Me: "Hi, it's me. I'm sending *Our Builder*."

I could hear the disbelief and relief in my wife's voice when she replied.

Wife: "You're sending *Our Builder*? Wow. Thank you."

As I sat in my remote operations centre, I waited for things to play out. Guess what, just like the movies, they did. *Our Builder* duly arrived, with reinforcements ('The Wolf' came alone) and based on the intelligence he had received from my remote HQ, he was able to, within no time at all, provide the required crisis management.

Heavy things were lifted, things were cleared and put out to dry and 'Our Builder' even took his top off (that wasn't in the brief I gave him, but he did arrive on scene wearing a white T-shirt so that was perhaps understandable).

I called my wife.

Me: "Everything sorted?"
Wife: "That was brilliant, Thanks for that."

If you haven't seen the movie *Pulp Fiction,* then you really should. To my mind, it's a classic. If you have seen the movie then you will understand it when I say, in terms of the role I played and being able to step up to the plate I was, '**On the M. £.$.@.+.R F.%.<.{.+.R!'**

The rest of my trip to Blighty went without incident, except to say that when it was time to leave, while at the airport, I went to buy what was my favourite newspaper. If there was one thing that I'd slightly missed, it was having breakfast while reading the newspaper. I used to be able to get my favourite English newspaper in Portugal, albeit at an inflated price, but now it was not available.

Anyway, I thought I would treat myself. It was the last time. In the 2 years I had been in Portugal, the price of it had risen from 50p to 65p. I didn't bother being all Yorkshire about it, I was just glad that I was getting on a plane to go home.

Almost Built a House in Portugal

I was hoping to have some poetic verse about arriving back in Portugal, referencing perhaps a well-known classical Portuguese poet while conjuring up images of sun, sea, sand, surf and something else beginning with 'S' that I couldn't quite think of.

Well, I don't know any Portuguese poets or poetry, but I do know that the sight of my wife at the arrivals gate, with her beaming smile, was all the poetry I needed. She had even gone to the trouble of wearing a fancy frock, which went some way to providing all the rhyming couplets and symbolism a working class lad, like myself, needed.

While I'd been away, I had had both the architect and the builder on the phone to me. I'd been able to field their questions and handle things, or refer them to my wife, but being back on the ground gave me the feeling (rightly or wrongly) of once again being in control.

Whether on a day-to-day basis, my nearly ever-present face on site had any effect on the guys working there was possibly up for debate, but it did allow me to see each stage of the construction, ask perhaps irritating questions, and check whether what had been asked to be done was actually done.

I'm not sure if this is true of all builders, Portuguese builders, or just the guys on our project, but during the course of our build, I often had the feeling if things weren't what they normally did, we had to check to ensure we got what we asked for.

As well as being available to check things out, come up with bright ideas that, although cost money and took you way over budget, couldn't be ignored once you'd thought of them, I was also on hand to continually see things that needed to be done that hadn't been budgeted for.

We hadn't thought about an alarm system, the extra size windows, the extra windows, the necessary retaining walls, the barbecue area (which we thought was part of our original quotation and were suitably surprised and worried about the cost implications when we realised it wasn't), the steps to the rear of the house, the metal doors for the newly created basement, or the drainage, extra brick work, concrete flooring that were also for the newly created basement and all of the other things.

We'd already decided that we were going to get as much done as possible at this stage of the build and so now was not the time to be worried about money. In the words of the infamous pools winner Viv Nicholson, we were going to 'spend, spend, spend' and then afterwards, get used to bread, water and, as a treat every now and then, a little salt and pepper.

Having been building for almost a year, the house was looking close to being finished, which probably just heightened our frustrations at not being able to move in. The dogs at our rented accommodation had been in fine voice and if there was ever a reason for our new home having no neighbours, then these dogs were it.

We were ready to move out. On the flip side, the neighbour on the other side of our rented place, who we had nick-named 'Mr Bang Bang' (for reasons I'm about to explain), has perhaps made me not quite so absolute about not having neighbours.

From day one of living in our rented place, we were aware of someone who had a workshop next door to us. Our landlady, although having owned the house for several years, wasn't sure what they did, but there was one thing that was very clear. Whatever he did, it required things to be hammered sometimes from early in the morning to late at night and even at weekends. This hopefully gives you an explanation for our nickname for him.

One day, my natural inquisitiveness got the better of me and, during a chat in my best Portuguese, with the old lady who also lived next door, I discovered that Mr Bang Bang was her grandson who was a metal worker, producing doors, windows, and anything metal related.

Knowing that with our build, we would need all of the above, and with the hope of perhaps being able to utilise local skills, add to the local economy, and have a sneaky peek at who was partly responsible for our 'BANG BANG, WOOF WOOF' soundtrack that had become the theme tune to our renting lives, I decided to pay him a visit.

The corrugated metal sheets, that were the gates to the property, were a portal to what, depending on your preference, was a cross between a scrapyard, farmyard, storage facility, and everything in between. Everywhere you looked were things that were either salvaged or kept for years because they would come in handy.

Things for providing housing for either the chickens, turkeys, goats, cats, rabbits. Things that had found or been given a home. There was machinery for all types of farm work, building work, work I didn't know how to describe, motorbikes, quad bikes, two vans, one green and very old Peugeot 205, bales of straw, wire fencing and things I couldn't see because they were blocked, stacked or covered by the things I could see. Behind all this was Mr Bang Bang. (I now know his name but I like his nickname more.)

As I approached, Mr Bang Bang smiled. He was approximately 30 to 40 years old, 5' and 8" and was wearing an orange T-shirt with tears in it, blue denim jeans and heavy duty boots, all of which seemed one size too big for him. These were covered in dirt, grease or what looked like oil and he was surrounded by so much more equipment that made it clear the banging was more than just a hobby.

Slight in frame, with slightly curly brown and copper-coloured hair, his face and hands were also covered in oil or at least a black substance that made it clear that for living, he worked hard and long hours. The state of his hands didn't go unnoticed by me as he held one out to shake mine.

Luckily for me, Covid restrictions were still current so I politely made a spontaneous gesture that thankfully he understood to mean it wouldn't be wise, on this, and probably other occasions, to shake hands. Behind him was the old guy we had seen on a daily basis, who I presumed was his grandfather. To his left was his grandmother. Both grandparents looked at me with suspicion at first, him more than her, and as I introduced myself, I was relieved that Mr Bang Bang spoke excellent English.

His grandfather was, without any hint of understatement, a quintessential old school Portuguese man. I would hazard a guess that he was probably close to eighty or even older, 5' 8" with a toothless smile and a face that looked like he had lived and worked every minute of every day of his advanced years.

With that, you just know that his years' came with a knowledge of how to make the most of every season, plant, and natural resource that Portugal had to offer. He showed no signs of slowing down, and his flat cap, which seemed de rigueur for all older guys here, was permanently worn.

In the nearly two years since we've been here, I'd never seen him without it. I would rather not get into what his bedtime routines may or may not be but it wouldn't surprise me if he wore it in bed. After getting to know Mr Bang Bang, he told me his grandfather's previous life was as a builder.

My experience of his grandfather was of someone who now seemed to spend his time farming. He could be seen at all hours of the day, and late into the summer evenings, at the wheel of some sort of farming machinery tending one of the many fields he didn't necessarily own but seemed to have taken ownership of.

He was a portly guy, with what seemed like a MacGyver-like ability to make something out of nothing, fashioning what on the face of it seemed like junk or scrap metal, into a useful tool or money saving adornment for his house. When we first arrived, he seemed to look at us with a healthy distrust, or maybe it was just the fact that he didn't see or interact with strangers much.

The fact that we didn't speak Portuguese made it initially difficult for us to introduce ourselves. While we'd been here, we'd picked up the odd phrase and word, and I did try to speak to him but, beyond Bom Dia, Boa Tarde, Boe Noite (Good morning, afternoon, evening) I couldn't make out anything he said as everything sounded nothing like any Portuguese I had ever heard.

His grandmother, although a little younger looking, matched her husband for work ethic. In fact, they often worked as a double act, going as far as to her being lifted in the bucket of a JCB so she could reach whatever crop was in season.

Whenever I saw her, she was doing some manual labour type task that would have someone half her age puffing and panting in no time. As you would probably imagine, she had grey hair and a slight stoup. Her little frame, about 5' 4", which seemed always dressed in an apron type garment, belied her obvious strength.

Whether she was mowing, hoeing, picking fruit, marshalling goats, sheep, or tending to her traditional female chores, it always amazed me just how hard she worked. In Portuguese villages, like the one we were staying in, it was often the case that there is a wash-house type building.

In terms of labour-saving devices, for traditional Portuguese folks, things like washing machines were not the norm and the washhouses provided a place for the respective villagers to wash their clothes. They were stone white structures, complete with sinks and washboards and, like something from a bygone age, his grandmother could be seen there, doing the weekly washing.

I'd often wondered why it was that the grandfather had lots of machinery for his daily tasks but she still didn't have a washing machine. Yes, his machinery was probably as old, if not older than me, but surely they could get a washing machine.

One thing I'd noticed though was that her busy schedule never got in the way of her warm smile, which often greeted us as we waved or passed by in the car. In reality, and sadly, for many reasons, we'd probably never really get to know them but they had given us a glimpse of what life was and is like for some Portuguese people.

As well as that, for me, they project some of the merits and values of a simple life. The world had changed in the last eighty years but I honestly think they and their lives hadn't and I suspect they don't plan to change anything anytime soon. I hope they continue on for many years to come.

Mr Bang Bang was very approachable and softly spoken. As I described how his skills may be just the ticket for our building project, we were probably sizing each other up. We had often seen each other in the lane outside our respective houses and had always given each other a friendly wave, but this was the first time we were actually having a conversation.

He described his background as being self-taught in all things metal and, along with an education passed from grandfather to father to him, it was clear he had the skills and the knowledge that I needed but didn't have.

As with many Portuguese people, his workshop, or place of work, was very close to his house and in turn, his house was close to his auntie's, uncles and other relatives. I felt the more I explained about our project, the more we both opened up and relaxed in each other's company.

I'm not sure if it was the language barrier, because they couldn't understand what we were saying, or the fact our body language was giving off positive vibes, but very quickly both grandparents had relaxed their suspicious looks and had returned to what they had been previously doing before I arrived.

As we continued to talk, I was impressed by Mr Bang Bang's English but more importantly, I was reassured by his ability to guide me away from what I thought I wanted and steer me towards what I ought to be having. He gave advice based on his experience and based on ensuring I was going to get value for money and the best results.

I liked him and it wasn't long before we had an agreement about what work he was going to do for us and a date for work to start. We didn't have an agreed price but what made me feel even more reassured was that from speaking to me, he obviously felt he could trust me enough to pay him (after all he knew where I was living) and after speaking to him, I knew we had a skilled craftsman who would work in our best interests.

Of the jobs I discussed with Mr Bang Bang, one was the fencing that was to surround our land. As previously mentioned, our land was full of rocks. So many that if rocks were money, we would have been more than millionaires. At times the rocks were an issue, but as someone once said, 'If life gives you lemons, make lemonade', so we decided we should use the rocks to make gabion cages.

These are metal cages full of rocks which are used to make walls or retain earth. One of Mr Bang Bang's jobs was to make 26 cages each 1m x 1m x 0.5m. Also, we tasked him to make some metal gates and do the necessary metal work for the steel posts that would form the structure for our fencing. To say he did a good job at a fair price was an understatement and we had plans for more Bang Bang metal based solutions in the future.

My view on neighbours hasn't totally changed, and when you can hear them working for you and towards your dream, they certainly have their place, but with all things considered, rather than a shouty guy with too many dogs and a weird sense of animal welfare, and a gentleman and skilled craftsman, I was looking forward to our closest neighbours being expertly constructed cages full of rocks.

Throughout our build, alongside the Portuguese team employed by our contractor, we had also employed foreign labourers. These had invariably been men of Indian or Pakistani origin who, often through no fault of their own, had found themselves in Portugal, in a quest to find work and to be able to support their families back home.

Despite some (and on our project many) having professional, or high level qualifications in their own countries, these guys are often seen and treated as casual workers (without employment rights), who were often tasked to do unskilled or even skilled work.

They were then paid in accordance with the local economy. Portugal is not a rich country and wages reflect that. Despite my ignorance of global economics, we didn't think it was right, or seemed fair, that for an 8 hour day of hard physical work, these guys were typically paid anything between 35 and 50 Euros a day.

We paid them more. If you are ever lucky enough to take a similar journey to the one we've taken, and employ similar workers, we hope you will feel the same way.

We both still missed Marli.

Are We Nearly There Yet?

After nearly a year of building, and being able to see the shell of the house, we were just waiting for the windows. When we had watched all those housey programmes, it was always the windows that were the issue, seemed to cost the earth, and arrived late. Sure enough, it was the same for us.

Even though all protagonists had known about the house build and had known that our house was going to need windows, we were left with excuse upon excuse as to why our windows hadn't arrived and why it was no one's fault but just 'one of those things'. We had to be patient but the feeling that things could have been done more efficiently was, and still is, hard to shake.

When we started our build, and during all our romanticised discussions about what our new life was going to be like, we had decided to wait until the house was completely finished before moving in. A year later, after living in rented accommodation, with our barking neighbours, we were resigned to the fact that rather than the house being completely finished, what was most important was moving in.

We had to balance the dichotomy between quality workmanship and speed and, although speed was not necessarily a feature of our crack team of builders, in the main, they were producing quality work, so we took comfort in that.

So rather than a brand new sparkling house, we prepared to move into a work in progress, commonly known as a building site. Despite our frustrations, we had to admit our lives had totally changed for the better.

We were working less, spending more time together, and enjoying the predictable and warmer climate. We were also looking forward to opening our bottle of whiskey.

25 years ago, when we were younger, thinner, and full of youthful naivety, we had a holiday break to Ireland. At the time (and still to this day), we were both very much into drinking whiskey and we decided, in celebration of our love of a 'wee dram', we should take a trip to a distillery to see how our favourite drop is created.

In truth, based on our previous trips to Scotland, and the distilleries there, we knew how whiskey was made, so our Irish excursion was just an excuse, not that one was needed, to firstly, find out the difference between Scottish and Irish versions of this holy water, and more importantly, by partaking in a tasting session, to pretend we were cultured and discerning while simultaneously getting a bit tiddly. My perfect day out.

Along with tasting more than we should have done, we did actually learn something. Scottish whiskey is distilled twice, while Irish whiskey is distilled three times, which is one of the reasons for the often smoother taste of the Irish variety.

Anyway, as with all these types of trips, you went through the factory where you were spoken to about the processes during manufacture. You remember bits about it but forget most of it and then you are eventually led to 'The Gift Shop'.

Seeing all those whiskeys, and after having had more than our fair share of the samples they offered, we were ready to spend. Luckily for us and bearing in mind some of the bottles they had for sale, although I asked and tried to persuade them, they didn't do interest free credit.

If they had, we would probably be still paying for that trip. What they did have that year however, was an important anniversary and to celebrate, they had produced a limited batch of a Madeira finished single malt.

It wasn't cheap and we were young with limited funds, but we had also had all of the samples on offer and even managed to convince them we needed more, so we could concur with their assertion that the Irish stuff was indeed better than the Scottish stuff.

So feeling, shall we say, 'particularly cultured and more than a bit discerning' and in defiance of our bank balance, we bought a bottle. The bottle came in a presentation wooden case, with bronze-coloured clasps.

On the front of the case, it tells you everything you need to know to confirm that this is billed as something to be treasured. It's like when you get anything that is billed as premium, the experience of it starts as you look at it and then begin to unpack it.

Although I've never had an iPhone, I have always admired the packaging and presentation of Apple products and this was no different. As we opened the case, our experience of quality, craftsmanship and distilling excellence continued as our bottle, with its golden top and label, adorned with golden calligraphy, lay (no, scrap that) nestled in a cushioned bed of gold silk.

What had we done? We couldn't really afford this, but it was too late. We had bought it, surely we couldn't afford to drink it? We knew we couldn't just treat it like all the other bottles of whiskey we had previously bought and subsequently polished off.

This had to be for a special occasion. All we needed was the right occasion, something momentous enough to justify our near bankruptcy to buy it, but what could that be?

We returned from our trip to Ireland clutching our prize possession, however the knowledge that we had the spectre of an impending credit card bill had the effect of making us feel slightly less cultured and discerning and more young and careless. We decided to put our new investment in a cupboard and wait for the right moment to justify opening it and the dreaded credit card bill.

The bill arriving was a sobering moment and sparked a conversation similar to:

"Whose idea was this?"

"How much did we sample"?

"Bloody Hell."

"Shall we have beans on toast tonight, dear?"

In the intervening 25 years, along with worrying that it might get dropped, broken or stolen, we had occasionally opened our cupboard and stared at the wooden case, the bronze coloured clasps, the golden calligraphy, cushioned silk bed and our nestling bottle.

Lots of things had happened since we bought it, we got married, bought a house we couldn't really afford, had some professional successes, and failures, a PhD, etc., but nothing ever seemed like the right occasion to justify breaking that golden seal.

On deciding to move to Portugal, it was decided that the right moment to enjoy our investment was when we built our house. The 25 years had flown by but the moment when we could finally open our bottle of whiskey was approaching.

In our attempt to push forward our new Portuguese idyll, we had planted our first crop of vegetables and they were now starting to poke their heads through the soil and rubble that was our home and garden.

My raised beds were providing a plush new home for our developing home grown produce and despite the cigarette ends the builders kept leaving everywhere, our garden was beginning to take shape.

We could see where things were going to go and we could see how naive we had been when deciding to buy a big plot. It was going to cost a fortune to do it how we wanted. Every trip to the 'Mecca' that is *Leroy Merlin*, just gave us more ideas and brought home the fact that this was going to be a long, long, long term and expensive project.

The final few months before we finished the build, or in our case, moved into a building site, were the longest months of the whole project. When we just had a plot of land, it was just that, a dream or a vision, but as soon as you start the build, then every day seemed like a day too many before we could actually move in.

The final few months did provide some highlights though, including our trip to buy 'THE TVs'. For months, we (OK, I) had been walking past the electrical shops, doing my internet research, OLED, or the other type I've already forgotten, which brand, what features, what size.

When the moment came, although I enjoyed it, it was really easy and a bit of an anti-climax. We just went into the shop and said, 'can we have two of those please?' As it happened, they only had one of the ones we (OK, I) wanted, so we eventually went with my original choice and one that had a really good offer on it.

Basically, we just bought two really big TVs, because at the end of the day, they were all pretty much of a muchness and they all had features you'd never ever use, although now that we have them, whoever invented 'Airplay' definitely deserves a sip of our whiskey.

My wife's birthday was fast approaching and, apart from it being another opportunity to remind her that she is older than me and born in a different decade, it was also another opportunity for us to set an arbitrary deadline for the completion of the house.

The wait for the windows coincided with one of the worst periods of storms in recent Portuguese history. Even worse than the storms I told you about when we moved our furniture over. This meant that while the house was open to the elements, the elements took full advantage and deluged our house in (what I'm choosing to over dramatise as) biblical amounts of rain.

The site was completely waterlogged, impossible to access and the concrete floors, we had been so precious about having and protecting, were being tested to the max. We had questioned our builder about the prudence of laying the floor before the windows were in but he assured us (or is that gave us some flannel) about it being OK and that the windows would be arriving shortly.

In hindsight, our eagerness to get things done probably allowed him to convince us that it wouldn't be a problem. It was a problem. As we sat in our rented accommodation peering through rain-soaked windows at the sheets of rain, the incredible bolts of lighting and hearing thunder which gave credence to the theory surrounding God moving his furniture, all we could think was, 'the floors, our beautiful floors'. In reality, even if the windows were ready, the weather was such that they could not have been installed anyway.

From the start of the project, we had set ourselves targets. We had seen all those that had gone before us and had seen how their targets had just become milestones by which failure could be measured and we were determined that our project would be different.

In reality, as we were nearing the end of our build, looking back, every single target we had set ourselves had not been achieved and each target had come and gone. Moreover, it felt like each target had gone from being a gauge for success to being a self-crafted stick, which regularly beat us over the head to a chorus of 'what made you think you were so clever that you would be any different?' I know that's not a particularly catchy title for a song, but its awkwardness perhaps sums up how we had felt things had gone.

Another refrain that is often heard when people build their own home is 'We'll be in for Christmas'. Well, Christmas was fast approaching and bearing in mind we had not received a memo from Mr and Mrs Claus informing us that, on account of our build, they had taken the decision to postpone Christmas until we had finished, it was looking increasingly like there was no chance of us being able to look forward to our membership of the 'In for Christmas Club'.

We were so looking forward to membership and we had so many plans for the big day, but we had to be realistic. We were going to be spending another Christmas in our rented place. In the scheme of things, we knew we were very lucky.

Our land lady had kept her word and had never once mentioned or even hinted that we had out stayed our welcome. In fact, she had even resisted the temptation of asking how our build was going just in case it appeared like she wanted us out.

We had been so lucky to find her and, truth be told, she had been lucky to find us and so we knew there was no pressure on us. Throughout our build process, our land lady had had her own ups and downs and during these, we had been there to help, console, and cajole and so I think, not only did she enjoy having us, but she would also eventually miss us (or at least my wife!) when we left. Nonetheless, we were desperate to move out and into our *NEW HOUSE.*

Christmas day arrived and you guessed it, we woke up in our rented accommodation and what's more, neither of us found our *In for Christmas* club membership card under the tree. To tell you the truth, in the entire time we had been together, some 20 odd years, my wife and I had never had a Christmas tree, so we were never going to find anything under a tree that didn't exist.

I'm not really sure why we never had a tree, although it may have something to do with not having had children but, tree or no tree, we were disappointed that we hadn't made it for the customary deadline. The windows (well, most of them!) were eventually fitted on 23rd December.

To console ourselves, we decided to take a trip to see our nearly completed house so we could open a bottle of champagne, pat ourselves on the back for how far we had come and begin planning for next year and our first Christmas in our new house. As we arrived on site, we were both full of admiration for each other and our architect. The house looked amazing.

There wasn't as much admiration for the builder though, seeing as we were not in the damn thing yet, but we knew it would only be a couple of days so we decided to cut him a little bit of slack. We were happy and full of good spirits as we put the key in the lock.

Walking around, it felt as though we were in our own wonderland as we each told the other about our plans for furniture, colours, room arrangements, landscaping ideas and all the other things we had only ever seen on TV and read about in magazines. Now, we had our own finished (well nearly) house and we were going to be able to be just like the couples we had seen and read about.

After having been around the whole house and, just before the champagne cork flew, we decided to take a look in our newly created basement, which was never planned but was quickly becoming a great addition and had allowed us to store the majority of our furniture and belongings as we waited for the windows.

We turned the lock on the (what we now know was an overpriced) door. The storms we had experienced over the previous two weeks had left us a gift. A flooded basement, complete with at least six inches of water, ruined furniture, books, clothes, shoes, tools, and keepsakes that mean nothing to anyone else except us.

For the metrically minded among you, and seeing as we were in Portugal, I know that should have been approximately 15 cm, but this was no time for a continuation of our assimilation into Portuguese culture. It was all hands on deck to save what we could.

Any slack the builder had been enjoying as we walked around upstairs had most definitely tightened and as we bucketed, mopped, and wrung out, it was fair to say we were wet, the air was a deep shade of blue, the builders parentage and competence had been very much questioned and the champagne had been put back in the car.

To say we were crest fallen was more than a slight understatement. It wasn't supposed to be like this and especially not on Christmas day. As we finished salvaging, we were both angry, frustrated, and a few pieces of furniture, etc. lighter.

We drove back to our rented apartment in near silence as we both processed what had just happened. Had we made a mistake in doing the basement? Had we made a mistake with the builder? Was this the start of never ending problems? How much was this going to cost? Just how much had we lost?

Would the builder step up and make the necessary repairs? It was fair to say that the rest of the day wasn't that enjoyable. We were probably both to blame and although we shouldn't have let it, it ruined our Christmas. They do say however that 'every cloud has a silver lining' and I would like to thank 'they' because on this occasion 'they' were right.

In hindsight, we were glad we didn't get our *In for Christmas* membership card because if we had, our first Christmas in our new house would have been a disaster. This way we had a chance to discover this problem, set about dealing with it and work on getting over it.

It also gave us time to calm down before we discussed our Christmas day activities with our builder!

Portugal

We had had nearly two years of planning and over a year of building, but the day had finally arrived. 27th December. We were moving in! The house was nowhere near finished but it was watertight (ok mostly watertight). Our van 'Dave' had come into its own during the moving of our furniture, etc. and it was called upon once again to transport the final few remaining things.

As we said goodbye to our apartment, it seemed a little bit surreal as we were finally doing what we had been thinking, planning and talking about doing for so long. As we drove out of our rented driveway, and looked in the rear view mirror as the electric gates closed behind us, we looked forward to our own electric gates opening and driving on to our very own, albeit unfinished, driveway.

We had come to the end of a chapter in our lives, a chapter that at times seemed like it would never end, but a chapter we knew we could look upon fondly because it was the preface to a new and exciting story.

I actually can't remember which one of us put the key in the lock for the first time, but on moving in day, I gave my wife the privilege. The rest of the day was just a blur of trip after trip to and from Dave and finding places for everything.

Box after box, bag after bag all accompanied with a pride in what we had so far achieved and a joyous expectancy about the jobs still to be done, the decisions still to be made, and the years ahead living a life happily ever after.

As with most big projects, you think that when they are finished, then you'll be finished. In reality, when you finish, at the same time you actually start something and this was no different. We were starting a new life with new challenges (starting with the blooming basement) and we were proud of each other, impressed with each other and, by the end of the day, absolutely knackered.

Things were everywhere. The house was a mass of boxes, some of the window openings were boarded up, not all the bathrooms were finished, we had no kitchen, no heating, our bedroom couldn't be used because firstly, it was full of building materials and secondly, we didn't have the energy to make the bedframe, we had a makeshift kitchen table, which was a combination of a plastic and cardboard box and of course, a basement that was still more than damp, but we were in.

We also had no swimming pool. Oh, the hardship! The Christmas holidays meant that, for a few days, we wouldn't get the chance to speak to our builder about 'basement gate' but those few days did give us time to catch our breath and ensure that the house was well and truly christened and then, just for good measure, christened again. It also gave us some time to reflect on the whole process so far.

We had started this thing with a dream partially based in reality. On reflection, that reality was supported by a naivety and idealism without which, we probably wouldn't have had the courage to do what we did.

At the same time, our naivety and idealism inevitably set us up for a rollercoaster ride with disappointments that more seasoned self-builders either knew how to mitigate, or never set themselves up for in the first place. You had to make plans and dream; otherwise how could you tell when things were going well? Or, as we frequently found, not so well.

You had to have a plan so that when someone came along and showed you a better plan, you knew there were going to be improvements. Conversely, when someone came along and suggested a worst plan, you could feel proud of yourself for being right in the first place.

You need to be idealistic so you can aim high and achieve what *might* be achieved. At the same time, you also have to be realistic so that you can achieve what *can* be achieved. You have to stay true to yourself to get what you want, but you also have to realise that what you thought you wanted, might not be want you need.

There is, of course, the worry of actually getting what you wished for. There is no right, but there is definitely wrong, and irrespective of how much control you think you have, because you have to see into the future, what you really only have is all the responsibility for the end result.

You are at the mercy of others, with a reliance on a shared understanding and sense of honour. It all costs more than you planned for and, in our case, more than you have. (Incidentally, the extras we did have been worth it). You will see what you can't have, and you will see what you need but don't necessarily want to have to pay for and you will be constantly balancing between the two.

You will be impatient, while accepting that quality cannot be rushed, and you will ask for patience when being rushed.

There will be times of self-doubt, over-confidence, ignorance, knowledge, frustration, and sheer joy and after considering all that, although we have no immediate plans, I'd do it all again in a heartbeat.

The best thing (OK, second-best thing) had been seeing my wife grow and blossom revealing a steeliness, that I always suspected was there, and seeing our relationship strengthen through all of the uncertainty of the past few years.

I had seen many sides to my wife (some I'd like to see less of), but whenever I had waivered, there she has been and I hope she feels the same.

There had been some tense times, some raised voices, followed by (at least on my part) some quiet periods of reflection. There had been lots of giggles and out and out belly laughs and I think we agreed we were staying together if only to eternally annoy each other.

I hope I've learned a lot about myself, and other people, and I hope I've grown in confidence. I also hope I keep my idealism while remembering to give due respects to its equal, realism.

The best thing? This had to be two-fold. Surpassing all that had gone before with just the right blend of traditional and experimental flavours, and a chef so good he created something new each time we went, we are pleased to announce we have found Maharajah's, our new curry Mecca, HQ for future date nights, mad cap ideas and tomfoolery. We'd also built a house and now (with clichés in a state of readiness), the journey of building a home starts.

Although this is my last chapter, we are looking forward to the next stage of our journey and all that it brings, with realised plans and developing ideas, with ups and downs, and a dry basement. Our house will get there and there is still lots to do.

Nonetheless, irrespective of any developments or additions, our future home would always have one thing missing. Marli didn't get a chance to perfect her 'sunshine gait' on our soon to be re-laid patio. It was a long story but basically, along with quite a few other things, it had become apparent that our patio refused to be taken off the 'not done properly the first time' list.

We would never see Marli enjoy our 360-degree panoramic view of the hills of Sao Bras de Alportel but then I think back to when it was just date night, late night and early morning conversations about driving a cat to Portugal and building a house when we get there.

We did it.

Milton Keynes UK
Ingram Content Group UK Ltd.
UKHW020617281123
433366UK00014B/304